How to run any organization

Also by Theodore Caplow

How to run any organization

MANUAL OF PRACTICAL SOCIOLOGY

Theodore Caplow
University of Virginia

THE DRYDEN PRESS
Hinsdale, Illinois

Published simultaneously in Canada by Holt, Rinehart
and Winston of Canada, Limited.

Library of Congress Cataloging in Publication Data
Caplow, Theodore.
  How to run any organization.

  Bibliography: p.
  Includes index.
  1. Management. 2. Organization. I. Title.
HD31.C343   658.4   75–21493
ISBN 0–03–014911–8
ISBN 0–03–014886–3 college ed.

FIRST EDITION

Printed in the United States of America

Grateful acknowledgment is made to the following
for permission to quote or adapt from the publications listed:
Methods Press, from *Modular Management and Human
Leadership* by Frank F. Pieper. Copyright © 1958 by
Frank F. Pieper.
Harvard Business Review, from "The Employee Performance Record: A New
Appraisal and Development Tool," by John Flanagan and Robert Burns,
September–October 1955, vol. 33, no. 5. Copyright, 1955, by the President
and Fellows of Harvard College.

7 8 9   059   9 8 7 6 5 4 3 2

Contents

Introduction

*In authority, in power, in charge, in control,
in command, at the head, at the helm,
at the wheel, in the saddle . . .*

EXCERPT FROM *Roget's Thesaurus*

What this book is for

One evening last winter, my wife, Christine, who had just taken over the temporary management of a small social agency, looked across the room and asked me to give her the titles of two or three manuals of management from which she could find out how to go about her assignment in a scientific way. I said that I didn't have the titles at the tip of my tongue but would look them up the next day. In the decade since my *Principles of Organization* was published, I had gotten a little out of touch with the hortatory literature of management and welcomed the opportunity to find out what was now available.

The search for those titles took much longer than expected and led directly to the present book. I was able to put together a list of excellent books, ranging from old standbys to recent best sellers (the list is given at the end of this book), but none of them really answered Christine's request for a short, easy handbook that would help her to run a small organization successfully and to avoid damaging mistakes while doing it.

The books I found were both too general and too particular for her purpose: too general in attempting to cover the entire field of managerial behavior, including relations with superiors and equals, and all sorts of topics not directly related to the problems of an individual who has primary responsibility for an organization; too particular in emphasizing the management of giant bureaucracies, like General Motors or the Department of Defense, while having little to say about running a social agency, a retail store, a basketball team, a summer camp, a local post office, a merchant ship, a public school, a parish church, or an underground newspaper—even though such organizations are likely to be taken in hand by inexperienced people who need instruction in the art of management, whereas the principal executives of General Motors and the Department of Defense have probably acquired some familiarity with the subject during their long careers.

Many of the books on the original reading list were written by serious scholars to present and defend their own theoretical discoveries. That is just as it should be in a field of study where many basic questions are still unsettled, but for a reader who wants practical advice, it is more useful to read about matters on which there is general agreement than to become involved in the controversies of experts. Fortunately, there is more than enough solid knowledge about the sociology of organizations and the psychology of management to fill a much larger volume than this one, and if at times we shall seem to skip lightly over some highly debatable issues like the connection between organizational structure and decision-making, it is not to deny their importance or to pretend to more certainty than the existing state of knowledge allows.

The purpose of this book is to help the man or woman responsible for running an organization to do the job in a way that fulfills the organization's collective purposes, satisfies the manager, contents his followers, and confuses his enemies, if any. The discussion will be limited to the problems of running an organization and will not attempt to cover the problems of being a good subordinate, even though it is obvious that running an organization that is part of a larger organization requires one to be a subordinate as well as a leader. But even if the two roles are entwined, they are distinguishable. In this book, we concentrate on the problems that belong to the managerial role.

What is an organization?

An organization is a social system deliberately established to carry out some definite purpose. It consists of a number of people in a pattern of relationships. The pattern is not entirely dependent on the particular persons who belong to the organization at a given time. The organization assigns a *position* to each of its members, and the incumbent of a position has a set part to play in the organization's collective *program*. Every organization has a program—a set of planned activities that can go well or badly. If they consistently go well, the organization thrives. If they go badly, it disappears or is restructured for another try. The manager of an organization is the person who has the primary responsibility for making its activities go well.

As organizational program always involves considerably more than one central activity. Whether the central activity is a production process, a game, a fight, or a ceremony, the organization must also maintain its internal structure, keep its members happy, and adapt to changes in the external environment. In addition, the manager of an organization has the peculiar and personal problem of establishing his own authority. In discussing his problems, we will take that one up first, since unless he can keep the right to manage, the other parts of the managerial assignment quickly become irrelevant. The first chapter of this manual, then, is called "Authority."

It does the organization little good, however, for the manager to establish his authority unless that authority is used to hold the organization together and achieve its purposes. Holding the organization together does not imply that all members of the organization will have identical goals and agree about how to achieve them, but it does require them to agree sufficiently for the organization to pursue its collective goals in a unified way. This limited agreement results from continuous communication up, down, and sideways within the organization. Most of this communication flows through established channels, formal or informal, and is modified in predictable ways by these channels. All this is discussed in the second chapter, "Communication."

But communication is not an end in itself. It is a means of getting the organization's job done, which is, of course, what management is all about. A manager is a person who supervises the work of others and can, by his own actions, increase or diminish their productivity. In practice, there are two quite different modes of supervision—direct and indirect—and they call for somewhat different strategies. In addition to the problems of routine supervision, there are all sorts of special problems that appear in any division of labor and interfere with the efficiency or the effectiveness of a work group. These matters are considered in chapter three, "Productivity."

The belief that productivity and morale are necessarily correlated is part of the folklore of organization. Like most pieces of folklore, it contains a grain of truth. Sudden increases in productivity are likely to stimulate short-term improvements of morale, and vice versa. But the general relationship between productivity and morale is more complex. As empirical studies in diverse types of organization have shown, high morale often accompanies low productivity, and crises of morale may be brought about by rising productivity. There is always some significant relationship between the output of an organization and the emotions of its members, but the relationship is far too intricate to suggest that productivity and morale are interchangeable. The managerial policies that sustain morale are described in "Morale," the fourth chapter.

No organization, however limited its goals, can safely ignore the larger social systems from which it draws its people and its resources. Every organization attempts to control the external environment, but no matter how large, rich, or sacred it becomes, it can not develop any real immunity to changes in the external environment. Some of these external changes are attributable to the organization's own activities; some result from long-term trends and can be anticipated in a general way; some are so surprising that they cannot be imagined until they have actually occurred. In a complex, modern society, this last category is nearly inexhaustible. The unanticipated effects of legislation, technology, political upheavals, moral fashions, migration and other forms of mobility; innovations in transportation, communication, and entertainment; the movement of prices, and the fluctuation of scarcities, now guarantee a fairly adventurous history to even the most insulated and reclusive organizations, such as craft unions and boarding schools. The problem of adapting an organization to external change is particularly challenging because external changes not only affect the conditions under which the organization pursues its goals but may also transform the goals. The problems that arise in this way can not be as neatly resolved as some of those discussed under other headings, but they are not hopelessly difficult, as we shall see in the final chapter, "Change."

These five topics—authority, communication, productivity, morale, and change—are the substance of this manual. We shall take them up in order, but before turning to the first lesson I would like to draw your attention to some basic principles of management.

Same basic principles of management

1. All human organizations resemble each other so closely that much of what is learned by managing one organization can be applied to managing any other organization. Every organization, for example, has a collective identity; a roster of members, friends, and antagonists; a program of activity and a time schedule to go with it; a table of organization; a set of formal rules partly undermined by informal rules; procedures for adding and removing members; utilitarian objects used in the organizational program; symbolic objects used in the organizational program; symbolic objects used in ceremonies and rituals; a history; a special vocabulary; some elements of folklore; a territory; and a method of placing members within that territory according to their relative importance. Every organization has a division of labor that allocates specialized tasks to its members and a status order that awards them unequal shares of authority, honor, and influence.

2. Every organization—except the very smallest—is a cluster of suborganizations of varying sizes. Each of these is an organization in its own right and has all of the normal features described above. Some suborganizations are departments of the parent or-

ganization; some are illegitimate factions of it; some are formally independent of the parent organization, like a union local in a factory, or attached to it temporarily, like an orchestra hired for an evening. The most important thing to remember about suborganizations is that their goals are never completely compatible with the goals of the parent organization. It is seldom possible, for example, to abolish or restructure a suborganization for the plain good of the parent organization without encountering resistance. On the other hand, it is quite impossible to manage a large organization without occasionally offending, damaging, or destroying some of its suborganizations.

3. The problems of managing a large organization are quite similar to the problems of managing a small or medium-sized organization, if only because every large organization is run by a managerial oligarchy which is, itself, a small organization—there is no other way to do it. Problems of communication, data retrieval, and public relations are necessarily more complex in a large organization, but there will be more people to help with them, too. Running a large organization should not require more time and effort from the responsible manager than running a small organization. If it does, something is probably wrong with the way his job is set up or with his personal style.

4. During any given interval in an organization's history, it will be growing, stable, or declining. Some organizations, such as industrial and commercial enterprises, normally strive for growth but do not always achieve it. Other organizations, such as exclusive clubs, attempt to avoid either growth or decline. Many organizations, such as legislatures and baseball teams, have a fixed number of members, although the number of assistants and supernumeraries can vary. Many organizations, such as social movements that are past their peak, continue to operate for long periods of time while declining in size. The task of management is easiest in a growing organization because growth itself—whatever its real cause—is usually viewed as a sign of managerial success and because the input of new resources occasioned by growth can be used to pay for mistakes. Managing a stable organization is a more difficult task and calls for a finer adjustment of means and ends, more careful decision-making, and more alertness to changes in the

external environment. The management of a declining organization may be easy or hard, depending upon whether the decline is regarded as inevitable. In the face of an inevitable decline, standards of managerial performance may be very low, as illustrated by the recent history of some railroad managements in the United States. In the case of a decline that is regarded as reversible, the task of the responsible manager is always difficult and sometimes impossible.

5. Most organizations find it easier to satisfy some of their goals than others, for reasons beyond their control. When this is the case, the manager's success or failure in one of his basic assignments becomes critical, while his performance of other assignments is overlooked or taken for granted. Maintaining authority is always critical, for example, in a prison or penitentiary; holding the organization together is what counts most in a civic association; the director of a summer camp is judged almost exclusively by whether he can keep up morale; the coach of a football team who can win all his games need not worry about much else. Thus, every familiar type of organization tends to develop managers who are overspecialized in the accomplishment of one assignment and who minimize the importance of their other responsibilities until this neglect catches up with them in the shape of rebellion, schism, bankruptcy, reorganization, or unwelcome advice from outside experts.

6. Many organizations develop crises from time to time. An organizational crisis is a situation in which the priorities of management are forcibly rearranged by some unforeseen combination of circumstances. The qualities a manager is called upon to display in a crisis may be quite different from those routinely required of him. College presidents are called on for personal courage, prison wardens are asked to show Christian charity, efficiency experts must respond to irrational sentiments, long-term planners are compelled to make snap decisions. Luck and skill play equal parts in the management of crisis. The skill can be practiced, but not the luck, so that while a few well-handled major crises may strengthen an organization and its leadership, a long series of crises will almost certainly ruin it. The manager who perceives his role as "putting out fires" is a poor manager and ought to be replaced by

someone who attaches more importance to fire prevention. The fundamental procedures for preventing organizational crises are early detection and the rehearsal of drills that transform crises into routine problems. This is more easily said than done, but is worth the doing.

1: Authority

There was trouble in the State of Lu, and the reigning monarch called on Confucius to ask for his help; when the Master arrived at the court, he went to a public place and took a seat in the correct way, facing south, and all trouble disappeared.

FROM A CHINESE CHRONICLE

Love, fear, and charisma

Opinions differ about whether it is better for a manager to be loved or feared by his subordinates, but to be loved *and* feared is best of all.

Fear is a normal reaction to a person who embodies uncontrollable power over oneself, who can reward and punish as he pleases. The courtiers of Henry VIII or the Grand Turk lived in a constant exhilaration of fear, knowing that the master with whom they associated daily could end their lives with a casual word. I have seen lieutenants literally paralyzed by the appearance of a brigadier general and professors backing away from a university president with profound bows. It is not at all unusual for foremen and choirmasters to arouse the same sort of panic among their people. I knew a chef so feared in his kitchen that the cooks' knees knocked visibly at his approach. Not to mention the Mafia dons

9

and high school principals whose stock in trade is their ability to scare people.

Love is another spontaneous reaction to authority. The love of armies for their generals has been one of history's strongest forces. There is always some love between a good teacher and a good class, and even between a good chairman and his committee. Many a modern executive would leave spouse and child, parent and friend, to follow his boss, and does so from time to time.

The talent for arousing fear and love in followers is called *charisma*. The term was invented by the great German sociologist Max Weber to describe a type of nonbureaucratic leadership, but charisma is abundantly displayed in bureaucratic organizations, too. We tend to think of it as a kind of natural gift, like musical talent, but the empirical evidence does not support this view. In some positions, such as the speaker of a legislature, nearly every incumbent appears charismatic; in other instances, it seems to be the combination of a particular personality and a particular position that generates charisma. A few of history's most charismatic figures—Mary Baker Eddy and Pope John XXIII come to mind— developed their charisma in extreme old age. There is no single constellation of personality traits we can associate with charisma. Some charismatic figures are marked by their enthusiastic vitality, others by their pale and rigid austerity; some are sociable, others withdrawn; some use their powers to win lovers, others avoid all intimate contacts. If we look at the most charismatic figures of a particular era, it is hard to discern any common traits except a measure of intelligence and energy. What other resemblances can be found between Abraham Lincoln and Robert E. Lee, between Churchill and Hitler, between President Kennedy and Chairman Mao?

But to return to management on a more modest scale, how is one to be both feared and loved by some (never all) of one's followers? What makes a manager feared is the reputation of act- ing decisively and ruthlessly when the interests of the organization, as he conceives them, are opposed to the interests of individuals. The establishment of such a reputation is partly a matter of style and partly a matter of substance. The appropriate style is that punitive measures are imposed promptly and confidently, without any visible interest in the excuses of the offender. One or two harsh actions of this kind can make a leader more feared than a whole reign of terror conducted in a more capricious manner.

The best policy to follow in developing a reputation for severity is to make all decisions that involve conflicts between the organization and its members according to fixed principles announced in advance and applied so consistently that each application takes on a didactic character. Nearly every organization, for example, must eventually deal with a theft of organizational property by a member, an offense that cannot be ignored without inviting trouble. It does not matter so much whether the organization's reaction is prosecution or expulsion or demotion or counseling, but it does matter that the full penalty be invoked in every case without much regard to extenuating circumstances or to such expedient considerations as the possibility of reprisal by the offender's friends.

Organizational love is even more predictable than organizational fear. For a manager to be loved, the organization's program must be successful, its success must be attributable to him, and he must have a reputation for acts of kindness to individual followers. Success is the essential element in this formula. Without it, the organization will not love its leader at all, although after conspicuous success has aroused an emotional attachment between leader and followers, that devotion sometimes persists throughout a subsequent period of failure. More often it does not. Winning football coaches and political candidates are loved despite bad habits and defective characters. The greater the organization's success, the easier it is for its leader to claim the credit and the less likely that his claim will be disputed. If the organization is extremely successful—the football team undefeated or the candidate swept into office by a landslide—it may not even be necessary for the leader to perform those small acts of kindness toward individuals which assure the onlookers of his potential goodwill toward themselves. If he is genuinely kind and sympathetic, so much the better; a whole body of anecdote and legend will grow up around him. If he is not, the myth of his kindness will spring up by itself or can be fabricated. Organizational success is the vital ingredient in this love potion.

We are, of course, getting a little ahead of our story. Before a manager can be feared or loved for his achievements, he must first assume his office, discover its powers and limitations, and exercise in fact the authority to which he is entitled in theory. This process always takes some time and causes some trouble. Let us look at it more closely.

Assuming the office

Leaving out those few managers who obtain an office by founding a new organization, most new managers are installed as successors to a former manager. The important elements in the pattern of succession are the strength of the predecessor and where the successor is found.[1] There are four basic situations, as outlined in Table 1: an outsider who follows a strong predecessor, an insider who follows a strong predecessor, an outsider who follows a weak predecessor, and an insider who follows a weak predecessor. The most promising of these situations is that of the outsider who follows a weak predecessor. In that case, the new incumbent is sure of a welcome but is not bound by his predecessor's policy or constrained either to imitate or to avoid his predecessor's style. The least promising situation is that of an insider who follows a strong predecessor. If he imitates the predecessor's style he will appear inadequate or ludicrous to those who knew him in a subordinate capacity, while if he changes the style and modifies the policies that have been working so well, he will seem foolish and perhaps disloyal. There is no easy way out of this trap. In the long history of hereditary monarchy, very few of the sons of highly successful fathers were successful in turn, except when the son was allowed to assume his duties gradually, under the tutelage and protection of his father, before the latter's disappearance from the scene. Philip II of Spain was thus introduced to power by Charles V and Marcus Aurelius by the Emperor Hadrian, two of the rare instances when

Table 1: Chances of success in various types of managerial succession

	Strong predecessor	Weak predecessor
Inside successor	Chances unfavorable	Chances uncertain
Outside successor	Chances moderately favorable	Chances very favorable

a great ruler was able to transfer power to an heir without loss of momentum. This solution requires more foresight, good judgment, and generosity on the part of the predecessor than is often to be found. Donald B. Trow's study of executive succession in more than a hundred manufacturing companies found that in a stable, family-owned company in which the manager's son was the potential successor, he was likely to be regarded as unfit for the job.[2] Without special preparation, the inside successor's best hope is to promise to imitate his great predecessor and then to involve the organization in a conflict, a merger, or some other adventure large enough to change its character.

The insider following a weak predecessor may do fairly well if he is the leader of a rebellious faction that undermined or overthrew the previous regime and if, upon taking office, he is able to act decisively toward the supporters of the old regime, removing them or winning them over, as circumstances allow. Unless he can do one or the other, his term of office will be short and unhappy The insider who succeeds a weak predecessor to whom he owes loyalty is in so hopeless a situation that only luck can save him.

The most interesting of the four situations is that of an outsider who follows a strong predecessor. It can work out well or badly, and the outcome is largely determined by the actions of the new incumbent. What he must do is develop a personal style that contrasts sharply with the style of his predecessor while retaining most of the policies that have made the organization strong. If his predecessor was a frosty autocrat, he can show himself to be friendly and outgoing. If bureaucratic rituals have been emphasized, the new style may encourage informal communications without disturbing essential bureaucratic procedures. If former policies emphasized growth, the new watchword may be stability. If the predecessor had a strong personal staff, it can be dismantled; if he worked alone, the time is ripe to recruit assistants. Such actions, baldly described, may appear whimsical, but they work in real life, as shown by such excellent case studies of succession as Alvin Gouldner's *Patterns of Industrial Bureaucracy*[3] and Robert H. Guest's *Organizational Change*.[4] The rationale for a dramatic change of style is partly psychological and partly structural. Psychologically, the new man cannot hope to escape unfavorable comparison with his successful predecessor unless he appears so different as to make comparison difficult. Structurally, a successor cannot hope to take over the hierarchy of support that sustained the authority of his predecessor and cannot expect to win over its key members, if only because they have been repudiated by his own selection.

In order to gain control of the organization, the new incumbent has to restructure the existing hierarchy and change the distribution of authority and influence in his own favor. He cannot do this by shifting people around on a large scale. He probably lacks authority to do so, and even if he has it, he cannot distinguish his potential friends from his potential foes at so early a stage. The existing hierarchy can be more tactfully, and just as effectively, reorganized by modifying a few key goals. If the prison's purpose is shifted from custody to rehabilitation, or the firm's primary interest from sales volume to profitability, or the college moves from selective to open admissions, it will inevitably follow that the key figures of the old regime lose influence and are gradually supplanted by people who are more beholden to the new regime. The danger in this strategy is that the people affected may perceive the threat and organize a mutiny. Whether such a mutiny is actually attempted and whether it succeeds in overturning the new regime is largely, although not entirely, determined by the timing of the new manager's actions, the topic to which we turn next.

The honeymoon period

Nearly every inauguration, from that of a pope or a President down to that of a restaurant manager or a platoon sergeant, is followed by a honeymoon period during which the new incumbent is almost exempt from criticism and his authority is almost unresisted.* It can be used either to settle in to the existing organizational structure or to introduce sweeping changes, but it cannot be used for both purposes at once. The new manager must make this

---

* The honeymoon metaphor goes back to Thomas Jefferson, who, contemplating the prospect of being elected President, wrote to a friend in 1796 that "the honey moon would be as short in that case as in any other, and its moments of extasy would be ransomed by years of torment. . . ."

choice very early. He need not announce it, but not to choose is a most serious error.

To make no innovations at all but carry on exactly in the predecessor's style is a practicable policy for an insider who follows a strong predecessor by whom he was trained and sponsored. It is also practicable in some organizations, like genealogical societies, where the manager's only responsibility is to preside over formal ceremonies. In most other organizational situations, the decision to leave well enough alone is highly questionable. The most prudent strategy for new managers, and the one they most often choose, is to lie low during the honeymoon, using the respite it offers to arrange furniture and files, choose assistants, study the organization, and meet the people who matter. The theory behind this strategy is that all serious decisions should be deferred until the new man has sufficient information to predict the effect of anything he does and enough contacts to provide good feedback. The great defect of this strategy is that it wastes the unique opportunity offered by the honeymoon to make major innovations without arousing major resistance. The strategy of lying low during the honeymoon may be appropriate for an outsider following a weak predecessor. His situation is so favorable that he need not hurry to establish his control of the organization, while at the same time he has a more acute need for information than an outsider who follows a strong predecessor with clearly defined policies.

The same strategy is clearly advantageous for the insider following a strong predecessor. If he enters office with the direct sponsorship of that predecessor, any changes in style or policy he introduces early in his term of office will be seen as a kind of disloyalty. If he takes office on his own, his initial authority will not be sufficient for him to innovate safely, and any innovation he attempts may become the occasion of a humiliating setback. His best hope is to lie low, cultivate friends and supporters, and wait for changes in the organizational climate.

The alternative strategy is to use the protection provided by the honeymoon to introduce sweeping changes, accompanied in some instances by wholesale dismissals or reassignments of personnel. This appears to be the optimum strategy for both the outsider who follows a strong predecessor and the insider who follows

a weak one, although for somewhat different reasons. The outsider
following a strong predecessor must establish his authority at once
or he may never be able to do so. The immunity offered by the
honeymoon gives him a chance to demonstrate authority by introducing major changes before the old guard has a chance to begin
the mutiny it will inevitably attempt. The only thing that limits his
role as a new broom sweeping clean is his ignorance of the organization and the danger that some of his innovations will have disastrous results. He can protect himself against this danger by
emphasizing changes of style and general policy and avoiding
projects that require detailed implementation. His reign of terror,
if he conducts one at all, ought to be highly selective and limited to
a small number of potential opponents. The other key figures in
the organization, having been edified by these examples, should be
encouraged and supported in every possible way.

The insider following a weak predecessor ought to follow a
similar policy during the honeymoon except that, since his position
is shakier and his authority more questionable at the beginning, his
program of innovation should be as comprehensive as the circumstances allow and should emphasize changes of policy over
changes of style. A selective reign of terror is inadvisable for
someone already involved in the organization's network of friend-
ships and antagonisms. Either he must attempt to remove all his
potential opponents, which will ruin the organization in nine cases
out of ten, or he must try to win them over by forgiving and
forgetting past differences. This policy, too, will often be ruinous;
but the insider following a weak predecessor is slated for trouble
anyway, and the odds, such as they are, favor a conciliatory approach.

Table 2: Recommended honeymoon strategies for new managers

	Strong predecessor	Weak predecessor
Inside successor	Lie low	New broom, emphasizing changes of policy
Outside successor	New broom, emphasizing changes of style	Lie low

Finding the purse strings

So critical is the honeymoon for a new manager that by the time it ends, either by the accumulation of petty issues or the eruption of a major crisis, his eventual success or failure may be already assured. It is much easier for him to guarantee failure by his own actions than to guarantee success, which is subject to factors outside his control. One predictor of a manager's eventual downfall is failure to secure control of the organization's finances by the end of the honeymoon. The power of the purse is the fundamental prerogative of management—in a government or in a glee club. The newly inaugurated leader who expects to be preoccupied by statesmanship or polyphony may be shocked to discover that money has become his principal concern and will remain so as long as he remains in charge of the organization. It is quite likely that he rose to office by displaying other abilities, and regards finance as the grubby business of bookkeepers and accountants; but he had better recognize that money is what management is mostly about and train himself quickly in his new trade. There is no way of managing an organization successfully without exerting effective control over its expenditures. Practically speaking, this means that the new manager of an organization must study its accounts until he is familiar with all the components of the organization's finances and knows all about the sources of its funds, how they are kept, how disbursements are authorized and audited, and how much authority he has with respect to each type of transaction. This course of study may be full of sad surprises, either because the organization is less solvent than it appears, or because fiscal control has drifted into other hands and cannot easily be recovered, or because a pattern of fixed expenses inherited from the past or imposed by outsiders limits the scope of managerial action. The unpleasantries, whatever they are, need to be learned, absorbed, and built into the framework of decision-making. In the usual case, the new manager who has done his homework and learned the location of the purse strings will have to engage in several sharp scuffles to gain possession of them. How to keep them in possession, once secured, is a later problem that requires close attention to the table of organization.

Tables of organization

A table of organization is a chart that shows all the positions in an organization and the relationships of authority and responsibility by which they are connected. The trick of describing an organization by such a chart, with its little boxes connected by vertical and horizontal lines, is relatively modern—the earliest known example dates back to around 1900—but the underlying idea is as old as the pyramids. Nearly every serious discussion of an organization, including the discussion a new manager has with friends or sponsors before he accepts the job, starts by laying out the table of organization. It has often been noted that the table of organization does not tell us everything there is to know about the organizational structure, but no one seriously expects it to do so. Among the omitted details are most of the relationships between people who have no authority or reporting responsibility with respect to each other, but must coordinate their activities anyway. Also omitted—by definition—are the informal norms which, in every organization, concentrate more authority in certain positions than the table of organization anticipates; and all the personal preferences, alliances, and coalitions, exchanges of favors, interferences by outsiders, and customary breaches of the rules that develop in any well-established organization.

What the table of organization does include, however, is fundamental and cannot be overlooked or forgotten by a manager without inviting immediate trouble. Nearly every table of organization has distinctive pecularities not shared by organizations of other types, or even by other organizations of the same type. Being a sort of social machine, it has in most cases been deliberately designed for its functions, and, like any other machine, it may be well or badly designed, cumbersome or streamlined, costly or economical, modern or antiquated. From the manager's standpoint, a good table of organization is one that makes his job easy, and a bad table of organization is one that makes it difficult. Since his first assignment when he takes office is the establishment of his own authority, his earliest examination of the table of organization will probably focus on the question of how much authority it confers.

The proper design of tables of organization is the most controversial topic in modern management theory. A fine summary of the principal issues can be found in Learned and Sproat's *Organization Theory and Policy*.[5] The principal points on which experts disagree are: (a) the relative advantages of centralized versus decentralized authority; (b) the desirability of unity of command ("one man, one boss") as compared to more specialized supervision; (c) the question of how much "line" authority should be exercised by staff personnel; (d) the relative advantages of directive and participative decision-making. Some of these issues are more apparent than real. Nearly all serious students in this field now agree that there is no single form of organization or style of leadership that fits all organizations but that, on the contrary, the functions performed by a given organization must be taken into account to determine whether it will run better on a centralized or decentralized basis, and under authoritarian or democratic leadership. Furthermore, many poorly run organizations need more centralization *and* more decentralization, more direction *and* more participation, all at the same time.

In the discussion that follows, we will consider the table of organization from the special standpoint of the responsible manager engaged in establishing his authority. His first assignment is access to all parts of the organization. The worst possible arrangement is that in which all contact between manager and organization is monitored by a powerful gatekeeper who can manipulate the flow of information upward and downward. Some marvelously inept managers, like Richard Nixon and Ferdinand VII of Spain, have installed such arrangements on their own initiatives. More commonly, a new manager inherits such an arrangement from a weak predecessor and may find it difficult to dismantle. When the outsider appointed to the presidency of the company described in Table 3 discovers that the comptroller, the legal department, the research director, and the heads of major operating departments report to the executive vice-president, he knows that he has only a fighting chance of establishing his authority. In a small organization like a retail store, an elementary school, or a social agency, the

Table 3: A poor table of organization, from the new president's standpoint

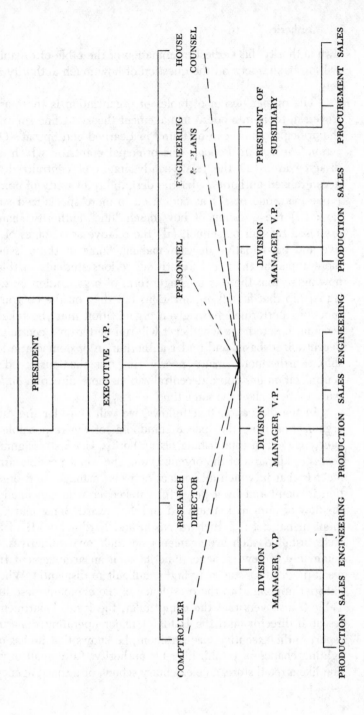

manager needs direct contact with, and some control over, every member of the organization. In a large bureaucratic organization, direct contact is not feasible, but it should be possible for the responsible manager to initiate direct communication anywhere in the organization and to punish or reward any individual in it. If these requirements are not met, the organization is partly out of control, but a degree of manageability is salvaged by giving the head of the agency power to approve or disapprove all appointments, promotions, and transfers. When even this limited prerogative is lacking, as in the factories of the French tobacco monopoly described by Michel Crozier in *The Bureaucratic Phenomenon*, the manager becomes a figurehead with hardly any influence on the enterprise over which he presides.

> . . . The director's role in the plant is small. Production goals are narrowly fixed by the central office. Processes are stable and change is extremely difficult. The director does not have the right either to hire or to fire; he does not even have the right to assign workers to various jobs. The only people who are really dependent on him are those in the extremely weak supervisors' group. His only chance of making his influence felt is to administer the rules in such a way as to diminish the constant squabbling their application brings, and, in that way, to inspire people with more positive attitudes toward production.[6]

Only the fact that his own job is so secure as to be scarcely affected by his own performance makes it possible for the director of such an establishment to continue in office with some equanimity.

From almost any manager's standpoint, the people below him in the table of organization can be divided into four groups: (1) personal assistants, (2) staff, (3) subordinate managers, and (4) rank and file. It may help in visualizing the relationship of these four categories if we point out who they are in two organizations of different types.

Consider a neighborhood church. The minister's personal assistants are his part-time secretary and his wife; the sexton and the organist are his staff; the choirmaster and the Sunday school superintendent are subordinate managers. The congregation makes up the rank and file.

Consider the president of the company shown in Table 4. His

Table 4: A good table of organization, from the new president's standpoint

personal assistants include an office manager, three secretaries, two assistants to the president, a receptionist, and a chauffeur; his staff are the company comptroller, the heads of the legal, personnel, and public relations departments, and the vice-presidents in charge of research and development, marketing and production. The subordinate managers shown in the table are group vice-presidents and presidents of subsidiaries. Lower managers and the rank and file are omitted from the table.

In tiny organizations, two of these roles may be combined in the same person. In a road-mending crew, for example, the timekeeper may be both the foreman's personal assistant and the sole member of his staff, but in that case he will have to be treated a little differently in each role.

The larger an organization, the greater the number of successive layers of management that are likely to develop until, in a very large organization like the United States government, most of the people with whom the chief executive deals, even among his personal assistants, have management structures of their own, including personal assistants, a staff, subordinate managers, and a rank and file. But this complexity is more apparent than real since, from the standpoint of any manager confronting the table of organization for which he is responsible, the same four groups of subordinates appear and present the same types of problems.

DEALING WITH PERSONAL ASSISTANTS

As the new manager examines the table of organization, he ought to discover that all his personal assistants are under his direct and exclusive control. They should not be required to report to anyone else or even to consult with anyone else except at his direction. Each of them ought to be beholden to the manager alone for pay and promotion, and subject to dismissal at his pleasure. A personal assistant who is too responsive to someone else in the organization poses a threat to even the strongest manager and should not be tolerated for longer than it takes to arrange a replacement. In the medieval French monarchy, the first thing that happened at the accession of a new king was that the former king's chamberlain came before the throne and broke his staff of office. By a sensible custom, he was never reappointed.

If it is essential that personal assistants be under no obligation to other persons in the managerial ambience, it is equally important that they not acquire authority over staff officials and subordinate managers. Because they enjoy daily access to the manager, know his secrets, and cont· his flow of information, personal assistants who are faithful and competent inevitably acquire more power than the table of organization assigns to them. It is one of the principal responsibilities of the manager to keep this power in constant check. This is done formally by keeping the rank, pay, and perquisites of personal assistants well below those of other people in the managerial circle and by a constant surveillance to make sure they are not abusing their informal authority.

In absolute monarchies and family-owned businesses, if the man or woman responsible for management lacks talent or inclination for the job, he may delegate his power to a personal assistant —a mistress or favorite like Pompadour or Buckingham; a private secretary like Wolsey or Richelieu; a body guard like Henry Ford's Harry Bennett. The theory behind the rule of personal assistants is that since the power they exercise is illegitimate and universally resented, they remain totally dependent on their patrons and can be dismissed without any trouble whenever the patron's enthusiasm cools. The experiment has been tried innumerable times with varied outcomes, but that story would take us too far afield. In the long run, the practice of ruling through a personal assistant seems to lead either to a revolution that overthrows the regime or to a new constitution in which the head of the organization becomes a ceremonial figure and the assistant, as shogun or grand vizier, becomes the legitimate manager.

DEALING WITH THE HEADQUARTERS STAFF

The most interesting part of a table of organization, from the manager's standpoint, is the section of it close to the top where the responsibilities of the headquarters staff are shown. His relationships with these key people are usually troublesome, since he is naturally dependent on them for information and advice but their individual interests differ from his own. Each of the key staff people is the advocate of a specialized approach to the organization's problems, for which he wants more scope than his colleagues are willing to concede. Each of them is additionally responsible for giving information and advice to subordinate managers, which involves him in a potential conflict with other staff officials and a potential conflict with the manager himself. At this level of the organization, more than at any other, the conflicting principles that enter into organizational decisions seem to be embodied in live protagonists: Mr. Skinflint the comptroller, Mr. Shakefinger the legal counsel, Mr. Spellbinder the marketing executive, Dr. Testube the research director, all with axes to grind.

A good table of organization includes certain specific provisions about the staff:

First, the major staff officials ought to be clearly unequal in rank, pay, influence, and other status attributes, since if two or more of them are nearly equal, their struggles for predominance will keep the organization in a constant state of turmoil.

Second, they ought to meet frequently with the manager as a council or cabinet so that most of their disputes can be resolved by direct interaction or by the persuasion of a majority opinion. If they meet frequently without the manager, they will probably come to perceive him as their common enemy. If they do not meet at all, they will use him as the rope in their tugs-of-war. In council, the manager's role as chairman enables him to develop a coalition against any malcontent without losing the benefit of the malcontent's advice, as in the famous case of President Lincoln and Secretary Stanton.

Third, the relationships between staff officials and the subordinate managers should be somewhat ambiguous. On the one hand, the manager cannot control subordinate managers if they are not fully responsive to line authority. On the other hand, even the most decentralized organization requires its departments to conform to certain fixed procedures, and these generally fall within the jurisdiction of the staff. The desirable ambiguity in the staff-line relationship whereby each party considers itself superior but fears to push the claim too far is secured by a number of conventional devices. Staff officials should be approximately equal in rank and perquisites to the subordinate managers with whom they deal, or perhaps a little lower to make up for the informal perquisites they acquire by proximity to the central authority. The people who carry out staff functions for a subordinate manager should report information to, and receive directives from, the headquarters staff but remain dependent on the subordinate manager for pay and promotion. A subordinate manager should never be required to go through the staff to obtain access to the manager, nor should the manager allow his direct channels of communication to the line to be blocked by staff officials.

Provisions for ambiguity invariably generate some friction between staff and line, but the definite predominance of one party or the other has graver consequences. When the staff is clearly on top, as in many social agencies, managers become grossly inefficient in their efforts to satisfy the incompatible demands of several masters. When the line clearly dominates the staff, as in some research institutes, the organization develops a remarkable capacity to resist or nullify managerial decisions.

DEALING WITH SUBORDINATE MANAGERS

Subordinate managers need to be treated very differently from staff officials, so differently that the rules a manager ought to follow are almost—but not quite—reversed when he turns from one group to the other. His basic objective in dealing with staff officials is to keep them from assuming too much responsibility. His objective in dealing with subordinate managers is to encourage them to assume as much responsibility as possible. The empirical evidence for this prescription is set forth at length in such books as Rensis Likert's *New Patterns of Management*,[7] Peter Drucker's *The Practice of Management*,[8] and Georges Friedmann's *Le Travail en Miettes*.[9] The unifying thread in these works is that the morale and productivity of an operating department can often be improved by giving it more independent responsibility for its part of the organization program. When subordinates are given more autonomy, their emotional commitment to the organizational program often increases in a dramatic way. On the technical side, their familiarity with operational details often enables them to run a given operation more effectively within broad guidelines than under tight instructions. One paradoxical result is that the manager who gives the fullest possible autonomy to his subordinates may find his power over them enhanced rather than diminished, because his

evaluation of their performance on behalf of the organization becomes vastly more important to them as their responsibility for
their own performance increases. Moreover, this phenomenon can
be carried down through successive levels of the hierarchy to the
individual worker, considered as the smallest possible "operating
department." On each level, the transfer of a substantial part of the
superior's decision-making prerogative to the subordinate tends to
increase the subordinate's commitment and contribution to the
organization and thereby to reinforce, rather than diminish, the
authority of each superior.

The secret that under certain conditions the more authority a
manager gives away, the more he has left, was discovered by Elton
Mayo and his associates in "human relations research" about half a
century ago.[10] It was the second critical event in the history of
scientific management; the first was the invention of time-and-
motion analysis by Frederick Taylor a generation earlier. The
Mayo discovery has given rise to innumerable innovations in the
management of large-scale organizations under such labels as
group dynamics, federal decentralization, conference methods, job
enlargement, sensitivity training, and participatory democracy. In
some experiments, a pyramidal structure of conferences and committees replaces the usual chain of command. In others, impersonal
measures of productivity are substituted for direct supervision.
Several influential movements like group dynamics and sensitivity
training have a psychoanalytic flavor; they identify the desire to
exercise direct authority as a neurosis and undertake to cure it by
group therapy. "Having a position of dominance," wrote Elliott
Jaques in *The Changing Culture of a Factory*, "stirs latent wishes
to dominate for the sake of power itself as well as for the requirements of the job. But, to the extent that dominance is used for
personal gratification, a profound sense of guilt ensues."[11]

The principle that authority can be enhanced by giving it
away is central to modern management, but it does have certain
limitations that prevent it from being universally applied. In many
operations, the need for precise coordination among the parts of an
organization is so compelling that it takes precedence over the
improvement of morale or even productivity. Most large organizations include operating units not fully committed to the organiza-

tional program and more likely to use an increase of autonomy to sabotage or abandon their tasks than to perform them with heightened zeal.

An even more fundamental limitation of the human relations approach is that subordinates as well as managers are capable of learning that the delegation of authority may be used to enhance a manager's power, and they may resist the manipulations of a manager oriented to human relations as stubbornly as the arm-twisting of an old-fashioned authoritarian. Many workers would rather be ruled by a drillmaster than by a psychiatric social worker.

There are some situations in which neither of these types of leadership is appropriate. Gordon Tullock in *The Politics of Bureaucracy* contrasts the situation of an infantry officer on the drill field with his situation in combat when he wants something other than simple obedience from his patrol commanders.

> What the captain wants from the patrol commanders is not the simple and uncomplicated obedience which we find on the drill ground, but something much more difficult to obtain. The captain wants the leaders of his patrol to reach decisions on the host of problems with which they will be confronted which will conform to his general strategy; but he cannot tell in advance what their decisions will be like. In this situation the company commander is making an attempt to multiply his mental powers by giving a task to subordinates which requires that they think and act on their own . . . .
>
> The patrol situation has the advantage over the parade ground situation in that far more decisions can be made by the whole organization because each of the subordinates must reach decisions in addition to the single superior. The disadvantage is that some of the decisions made by the subordinates will inevitably be contrary to the desires of the commander.[12]

There may be other disadvantages to the delegation of authority, as when subordinate managers have, or are on the way to acquiring, so much autonomous authority that the central organization is unable to suppress conflicts between them. Antony Jay writes:

> There's a constant danger of baronial war in any organization, and it is the first and surest sign of weakness at the top. . . . Frank Pace, who took over General Dynamics from its founder, Jay Hopkins, in

1957, found himself virtually a prisoner of his own feudal barons. His total head office staff numbered 200, in a company of 106,000 made up of nine divisions which were all virtually corporations in their own right. Most of them had been independent enterprises before they joined, and had their own separate legal and financial staffs and, of course, their tough baronial presidents. Pace decided to leave them more or less alone. "The only way to succeed," he said, "is to operate on a decentralized basis." . . . As a result of its feudal baronial structure, General Dynamics managed to lose four hundred and twenty-five million dollars between 1960 and 1962, the biggest product loss ever sustained by any company anywhere.[13]

When subordinate managers are weak, they will not work effectively for the organization, but when they are too strong, they cannot easily be restrained from fighting each other. A state of baronial warfare does not prevent mutinous coalitions against the ruler. Indeed, for reasons we will return to later, it makes such coalitions more likely.

The principle that a manager should delegate as much authority as possible to his subordinate managers obviously needs to be hedged with reservations. He should do so only if (a) his control of the organization's finances is secure; (b) the performance of operating departments can be objectively measured; (c) there is no obvious conflict of interest between a given operating department and the central organization; (d) the subordinate manager is not now and has never been an active candidate for the top position; and (f) the subordinate manager is not irremovable because of formal tenure or informal influence.

A headquarters staff, as we noted before, cannot function well except as a council, and it is a constant concern of the manager to encourage informal communication among his staff advisers. Nearly the opposite rule applies to subordinate managers—who are asked to be competitive without flying at each other's throats. Excessive communication among them multiplies the opportunities for destructive conflict and the parallel opportunities for improper coalitions. Most exceptions are only apparent. In the United States government, for example, the President's cabinet is composed of the heads of operating departments. In theory, it functions as an advisory council, but nearly every effective President has turned elsewhere for assistance in decision-making.

DEALING WITH THE RANK AND FILE

The remaining category that the new manager finds in the table of organization is the rank and file. In most cases, this level of the organization is much more heavily populated than the others— the pupils of a school, the workers of a factory, the soldiers of an army, the parishioners of a church, the clerks of a bureaucracy.

In many organizations there are two distinct levels of the rank and file: the lowest category of organizational functionaries and, below them, a category of clients—for example, welfare recipients —who must be considered as part of the organization because, unlike the guests of a hotel or the patrons of a theater, they are locked into the organization and subject to its authority.

The table of organization may omit the clients altogether, if only because they are not paid. But provided that the clients are routinely dependent on the organization and subject to managerial authority, they must be reckoned as part of the organization. Thus, a school has a rank and file of classroom teachers and another rank and file of pupils; a welfare agency has a rank and file of social workers and another of beneficiaries; a hospital has its rank and file of aides and attendants and another rank and file of patients.

Many rank and files have formal or informal representatives who represent their interests vis-à-vis management—shop stewards, walking delegates, prefects, tribunes of the people, and outside representatives of various kinds. Rank-and-file spokesmen are nearly always omitted from the table of organization, but this does not in any way diminish their importance in real life, and the manager who does not find them on the chart must still find out who they are, what they do, what occasions bring them out, and what they expect from him.

In a small organization, like a symphony orchestra or an elementary school, the manager may spend a large part of his working day in direct contact with the rank and file. In a larger organization, like a university or a department store, the manager's contact with the rank and file is likely to be very limited, and, if he is sensitive, he is likely to suffer from a sense of isolation from his constituents and to rely excessively for information on his few routine contacts with low ranking members of the organization, like chauffeurs and elevator operators, or with the few other rank-and-file people he happens to know personally.

The reason there is so little contact between the manager and the rank and file in most organizations is that such contact is not required by the organizational program. The manager communicates with staff officials and subordinate managers who, in turn, communicate with the rank and file. William Whyte's classic study of a street-corner gang in an Italian slum in Boston (described in his *Street Corner Society*) showed that although the gang had only about a dozen members, the leader's relationship with the rank and file was conducted almost exclusively through intermediaries.[14] Even in an organization of this miniature scale, it was possible to identify the staff officials and subordinate managers through whom the leader's communications with the seven or eight young men who composed the rank and file were transmitted.

Although the relationship between the manager and the rank and file is minimal in many organizations, it is nevertheless important to both parties, and in a serious crisis the manager's ability to understand and to be understood by the rank and file may be a crucial factor.

For the rank and file, the responsible manager is a living symbol of the organization's collective identity. Any honor or disgrace he incurs affects them all. Even the manager of a supermarket has some dim trace of the aura that surrounds monarchs, ship captains, senior partners of law firms, and museum curators. He may still continue to command the adherence of the rank and file if he is corrupt or cruel or technically incompetent, but he will lose them at once if he shows any sign of not taking the organization seriously or not caring about its reputation or not attaching any importance to his own prerogatives.

Besides his symbolic function as King of the Lions, the manager of an organization has practical duties in relation to the rank and file. He is, or should be, their definitive source of information about the organization's purposes and policies and whatever changes occur in them. He is, or ought to be, their ultimate guarantor of justice; that is, of the fair and equitable application of the organization's rules to individuals. In most well-run organizations, this means that some procedure is provided whereby an action that adversely affects any member of the organization can be appealed directly or indirectly to the top and can be nullified either for good cause, which is one sort of justice, or out of compassion, which is another sort of justice. Even if these executive prerogatives are seldom exercised, it is essential that they exist so that the organization does not appear to its rank and file as a heartless monster, incapable of remorse or sympathy. For similar reasons, in nearly all organizations the manager distributes promotions and rewards in his own name, if not on his own initiative.

The ritualistic nature of the relationship between the manager and the rank and file does not permit either side to indulge in much spontaneity. In particular, it impedes the flow of information upward. Every manager needs to know about some events at the rank-and-file level. For example, he would like to learn about any precipitous change in his own popularity, or the popularity of a subordinate manager, before mutiny erupts. It is almost as important for him to know when morale is exceptionally high and to understand how that happy condition has been produced.

This information will not come to him spontaneously in even the smallest organization. He must take active steps to obtain it. The method of Caliph Haroun Al-Raschid, whereby the ruler disguises himself and wanders among his subjects, is one of the best, but it can only be practiced by very self-confident rulers in very large organizations.

The difficulty experienced by many managers in obtaining a steady flow of information from the rank and file is related to one of the most fundamental problems of management: the tension inherent in the relationship between superiors and subordinates. To this irremovable problem and some of its partial solutions we now turn.

How to interact comfortably with subordinates

All of a manager's human contacts within the organization for which he is responsible are with subordinates. Within his organization he has no peers and no superiors. Unless he can get along comfortably with subordinates he will never be able to do his job well or enjoy it. Some people take to this situation more readily than others, but even very timid and self-conscious people can do very well in unequal relationships if they understand how the interaction between a subordinate and a superior in an organization differs from other human relationships and why a given conversation between a superior and a subordinate seldom evokes the same sentiments from both.

If we go into any organization and quietly observe the relationship between a superior and a subordinate for several weeks or months, we discover that most of their conversations are initiated by the subordinate, while most of the activity resulting from those conversations is initiated by the superior. Typically, the subordinate, having finished an assignment or run into a problem, goes to the superior and says, "This is the situation. What shall I do now?"—thus initiating a conversation. At the end of the conversation the superior says something like, "Why don't you try using the thingamabob?"—thus initiating an activity. The frequency *and* the content of these conversations is usually set by the subordinate, who has to balance a complicated set of constraints in doing so. The fewer of these conversations he has, the more autonomous he will be in carrying out his organizational tasks but the less help and protection he will receive from his superior and the less influence he will have on the organizational decisions that affect him. Faced with this Hobson's choice, most subordinates in most organizations choose autonomy and minimize contact with their superiors. An important minority of subordinates choose to maximize their contacts with their superiors because they feel either too weak to function autonomously or strong enough to gain more by close association than they lose by putting themselves under close supervision.

This pattern can be observed in a very wide range of situations, from the grade school class in which a majority of pupils avoid close contact with the teacher while a minority of teacher's pets seek her out, to the industrial organization in which most managers try to keep as much social and geographical distance as possible between themselves and the home office while a few appear there at every opportunity. The competent teacher will try hard to draw the isolated pupil closer and even harder to discourage the excessive dependence of the teacher's pet. A competent corporate manager will act very similarly in the parallel situation.

This is often more easily said than done, if only because of the sociopsychological illusion whereby we perceive extraneous conversation in a working relationship as a sign of friendliness. This perception is roughly accurate in relationships among organizational peers or in casual relationships where there is nothing to be gained from extraneous conversation besides the pleasure of sociability. In conversations between superiors and subordinates, although sociability plays its part, the participants always have ulterior motives, which makes it impossible for either party to interpret the sentiments of the other by so easy an index.

It is much better practice for a manager to measure the affection of his subordinates by their compliance with his orders rather than by their eagerness to fraternize with him.

Even with this austere criterion, a new manager is likely to misidentify the friends and enemies he has among his subordinates until he has had a long and varied experience with them. The superior and subordinate who interact frequently learn a great deal about each other, but each of them gets a different type of information. The superior gets a comprehensive view of the subordinate's performance because he sees it from above, can compare it with the organization's standards and the performance of the subordinate's peers, and has an unrestricted license to examine any aspect of the performance on behalf of the organization. The subordinate has a much hazier view of his superior's performance, much of which does not concern him at all, or is responsive to demands that he knows nothing about, or is judged by standards with which he has no reason to be familiar. The kindergarten teacher can evaluate the performance of her pupils quite easily, while the pupils have no way of judging the effectiveness of the teacher aside from whether they like or dislike her.

To compensate for the subordinate's tunnel vision with respect to the competence of his superior, he gets to know a great deal

Table 5: The mutual perspectives of superiors and subordinates

	Superior observing subordinate	Subordinate observing superior
Evaluating performance	Has much information	Has little information
Explaining motives	Has little information	Has much information

about his superior as a person without being required to reveal very much about himself in return. The superior ordinarily has no means of obtaining information about the habits or attitudes of a subordinate except by unaided observation, and what that observation can yield is severely limited by the subordinate's inclination to dissemble emotions and conceal events to which the superior might react unfavorably. The superior has less motive for personal concealment, since the subordinate's judgments are less threatening to him than his own judgments to the subordinate; but even if he wants to conceal himself, he has no way of shutting off the subordinate's exchange of information with other people in the organization to whom the superior is an object of constant interest and observation.

All that a manager can do about this basic situation is to follow certain counsels of prudence that take into account this disparity of perspective between himself and his subordinates. One such counsel is for him to mistrust his own opinions and judgments about subordinates in matters that are unrelated to their work or go beyond it. He cannot ever tell with certainty, for example, whether his cashier is honest out of conviction and lifelong habit or only to keep up appearances. Nor can he ever hope to understand the office love affairs that are crystal clear to everyone else in the organization. He ought not try very hard to participate in the organization's network of gossip and news, since at best he will remain ignorant of matters that everyone else knows about, and at worst his participation in the grapevine could be used to manipulate his judgment of people and events. On the other hand, he needs to remember that, while he cannot see through the veils worn by his subordinates, his own face is always under scrutiny from multiple points of observation, so that the attempt to present different faces to different people within the organization may expose him to ridicule.

There is another built-in imbalance in the emotional exchange between a superior and a subordinate. Under most circumstances their interaction makes much more difference for the subordinate than for the superior, if only because the subordinate has more to hope for by way of reward and more to fear by way of punishment. The sentiments of superiors to subordinates normally vary from friendly to hostile, while the sentiments of subordinates to superiors are often ambivalent, including both friendly and un-friendly feelings at the same time.

Of course, this pattern may be reversed or modified in particular cases. There are traces of ambivalence in every cooperative relationship, and instances of acute ambivalence may occur on either side of a relationship. By and large, however, the greater emotional vulnerability of subordinates and the susceptibility of subordinates to ambivalent feelings about superiors are reliable tendencies that need to be reckoned with in every type of organization. The reasons are almost self-evident. The subordinate is, among other things, an instrument for the achievement of the superior's purposes and is liked or loved if he fulfills that function and disliked or hated if he fails to do so. The superior, by contrast, is usually a source of both rewards and frustrations for the subordinate, and in both of these capacities he influences the subordinate's happiness more than his own is affected in return.

The usual reaction of a normally ambivalent subordinate is to display his affection and conceal his resentment in the presence of that superior. When there are a number of subordinates in the same situation, they will probably compete in expressing love and loyalty to the superior's face, but exchange their grievances behind his back.

There is no need for a manager to be alarmed by this prospect. It is a wholesome condition and will do him no harm provided he does not allow himself to be lulled into the illusion that he is universally loved. That illusion—the occupational disease of tyrants—is certain to get him into trouble sooner or later when he discovers perfidious thoughts among his followers or counts too heavily upon their loyalty in a crisis. "*Et tu, Brute*" is the perennial complaint of managers who do not take the ambivalence of their subordinates into account. The wiser ruler enjoys and reciprocates the expressions of devotion he continually receives, but omits them from his tactical calculations.

TAKING ACCOUNT OF THIRD PARTIES

The relationship between a superior and a subordinate is further complicated by the curious catalytic effects that occur in such relationships in the presence of third parties, especially when the third parties belong to the same hierarchy. The general pattern of these effects is summed up in Table 6, although there are innumerable variations and nuances.

The first column of the table shows what happens to the interaction between a superior and a subordinate in the presence of a third party. (The table refers in each case to a single third party; multiple third parties usually influence the relationship in the same direction but more forcefully.) As communication increases, interaction becomes more formal and less spontaneous, tongues are guarded, emotions are censored, and interaction approaches the minimum required by the organization program. The influence of third parties on interaction between superior and subordinate is dismayingly simple—the presence of *any* third party decreases it, although the intensity of the effect varies according to the identity of the third party.

The effect has all sorts of practical implications for the manager dealing with subordinates. Whenever he wants to hold a candid and unrestrained conversation with a subordinate, he had better arrange to hold it privately. When he needs to have such

Table 6: How the presence of a third party affects the interaction between a superior and a subordinate

Third party present	Communication between superior and subordinate	Authority of superior over subordinate	Emotional solidarity of superior and subordinate
Superior's superior	−	+	+
Superior's peer	−	+	−
Intervening subordinate	−	+	
Subordinate's peer	−	−	−
Subordinate's subordinate	−	−	+
Outsider	−	−	+

conversations with a number of subordinates, he had better see them one by one, even if that takes more time and trouble than he likes. The inhibiting effect of a third party is an automatic feature of the situation; it is not under the control of the people involved, and it cannot be suppressed by an effort of will. Busy managers often try to override the mechanism by ignoring the presence of a third party who is unavoidably present at a discussion but has no special interest in the matter discussed. The thing cannot be done. A conversation that pretends to be private is always less informative than one that *is* private.

The second column of Table 6 shows a somewhat more intricate set of effects. The pressure on a subordinate to conform to the authority of a superior is usually—although not invariably—enhanced by the presence of another superior, even of a person to whom the subordinate never reports. The bosses, he might say, gang up on him. This, too, is an automatic mechanism; when, as sometimes happens, it fails to work, the failure signals a breakdown in the hierarchical structure.

The presence of outsiders—those not in the hierarchy—has a similar, but feebler, effect on the interaction of superior and subordinate. The superior's authority may be reinforced, either because the outsider represents the larger social system to which the whole organization is subordinate, or because the exposure of an organization to an outside audience generates pressure to maintain normal appearances, as Erving Goffman shows in his *Relations in Public*.[15]

The presence of the subordinate's peers or subordinates has an opposite effect on the superior's authority, strengthening the subordinate's ability to resist, and restricting the scope of obedience the superior can demand.

Although this model is so simple as to seem a little simple-minded, it appears to work most of the time. An interesting study of a military unit by Reece McGee found that the bare ratio of superiors to peers and subordinates with whom an officer routinely interacted went a long way toward explaining how he was rated on efficiency and leadership.[16] In general, the more superiors the officer had to deal with, the harder he found it to appear efficient and to be rated as an effective leader; the more peers he had to back him up, and the more subordinates he had to help him with his assignments, the easier it was to make a good showing.

Most managers apply the principles stated above by intuition, individualizing their interaction with subordinates when they anticipate resistance and associating themselves with superiors and outsiders when they are not sure of obtaining compliance otherwise. Nonetheless, if the purpose of such a maneuver becomes apparent and the manager's uncertainty about his own authority is perceived by his subordinates, the maneuver is likely to fail. Juggling the audience to minimize the possibility that subordinates will defy his authority is something every manager has to do from time to time; the skill consists in doing it unobtrusively, so that the appearance or disappearance of third parties around the scene of action is attributable to other causes.

The last column of Table 6 shows the normal effect of the presence of third parties on the emotional solidarity of a superior and a subordinate. This follows a different pattern. The parties to an unequal relationship, like human actors everywhere, are drawn closer together by the presence of people who are different from themselves and potentially unfriendly, and are pulled apart by the appearance of rivals for each other's affections. In an organizational setting, the sense of solidarity between superior and a subordinate is strengthened by the presence of persons who are superior to both of them, subordinate to both of them, or altogether outside of their hierarchy. In the presence of a general, sergeants and privates stand together. Surrounded by civilians, the general and the enlisted men may feel a surprising warmth toward each other as fellow soldiers.

How to cope with coalitions

That extraordinarily original scholar Georg Simmel was the first sociologist to observe the systematic tendency of social groups made up of three parties—either individual or collective actors—to split into a combination of two against one. The combination of two is called a coalition, and the group of three in which it occurs is called a triad. The study of coalitions within triads fascinates modern sociologists because of the precision and regularity of the coalition-forming process under very diverse conditions and the ease with which very complex social systems can be reduced to triadic form for analytical purposes.[17] The point of such analyses is to understand how power is transformed into weakness, and weakness into power, by the shifting coalitions within a social system.

Triads are conventionally classified according to the relative power of their members into eight patterns, which seem to be found in all human societies. In relation to problems of management, the most important of these types is the hierarchical triad diagramed in Table 7.

Table 7: Coalitions in a hierarchical triad

NO COALITIONS ⟶ A

A DOMINATES B AND C, B DOMINATES C

WITH THE REBELLIOUS COALITION BC ⟶
BC DOMINATES A, B DOMINATES C

WITH THE IMPROPER COALITION AC ⟶
AC DOMINATES B, A DOMINATES C

WITH THE CONSERVATIVE COALITION AB ⟶
AB DOMINATES C, A DOMINATES B

In this triad, A is stronger than either B or C and dominates either of them alone, but A would be weaker than a BC coalition. When A is an organizational manager and BC are his two leading subordinates, A's major strategical problem is how to avoid the formation of the rebellious coalition BC. Almost any managerial situation can evolve into a pattern in which the manager confronts two subordinates capable of resisting his authority if they decide to combine against him. Captain Bligh's authority overawes Mr. Christian and the bosun separately, but if they combine against him, they are strong enough to put him over the side.

Even when a manager has overwhelming authority and cannot be overthrown, he must still reckon with the respectful coalitions formed by his subordinates, but the problems he has with those are relatively trivial compared to the problem of protecting himself against a rebellious coalition. In most organizations, the art of management consists to a very large extent of preventing rebellious coalitions. How is that prevention accomplished?

Long ago, Simmel saw how dangerous a triad with two equal subordinates can be for its more powerful member and how it automatically converts his relative strength to relative weakness by inviting the formation of a coalition which renders him helpless. Simmel's solution was to convert the triad with two equal subordinates to a hierarchical triad by making B and C somewhat unequal.

It was the general custom of the Incas to divide a newly conquered tribe in two approximately equal halves and to place a supervisor over each of them, but to give these two supervisors slightly different ranks. This was indeed the most suitable means for provoking rivalry between the two heads, which prevented any united actions against the ruler on the part of the subjected territory. By contrast, both identical ranks and greatly different ranks would have made identification much easier. If the two heads had had the same rank, an equal distribution of leadership in case of action would have been more likely than other arrangement; and, since there would have been need for subordination, peers would have most probably submitted to such a technical necessity. If the two heads had had very different ranks, the leadership of one would have found no opposition. The slight difference in rank least of all allows an organic and satisfactory arrangement in the unification feared, since the one would doubtless have claimed unconditional prerogative because of his superiority, which, on the other hand, was not significant enough to suggest the same claim to the other.[18]

Modern managers share the same perception, and it is rather unusual for two strong subordinates to remain substantially equal for any length of time. Even a weak, ineffectual manager can usually arrange to tip the balance of authority toward one subordinate or the other provided they have not already broken into open mutiny.

Of course, rebellious coalitions may also form in a hierarchical triad, with three unequal members, but a BC coalition is not as advantageous for the participants as it would be if they were equals. C, the weaker rebel, gains ascendancy over A by joining a BC coalition but remains subordinate to B within the coalition, sometimes trading one master for another. Depending upon local circumstances, this may or may not be desirable from his standpoint. He shares the unavoidable risks of rebellion equally with B but does not profit equally.

One alternative for C when offered a BC coalition is to form an AC coalition instead, for while he will be subordinate to his coalition partner in this case also, he will gain an ascendancy over B that he did not have before, without running any of the risks attached to rebellion against A.

The process whereby triads split into a division of two-against-one has been extensively studied in laboratory experiments. In the typical experiment, three subjects are asked to play a game or solve a problem that has been carefully arranged to make them unequal in power, and their behavior is observed through a one-way mirror and recorded by various instruments for later analysis. A series of such experiments by many investigators has confirmed the existence of a tendency for the two weaker members of a hierarchical triad to combine against the stronger member by forming a BC coalition. The probability of a BC coalition is not constant, however. It varies from one experimental game to another, and it can be manipulated by modifying the rules and conditions.

The reliable expectation in a hierarchical triad is that *some* coalition will be formed. The threat of a BC coalition is too much for A to live with indefinitely—particularly when he considers that

B stands to gain so much from a rebellious coalition that A may be willing to offer equality to C in order to gain C's adherence. At the same time, B is acutely aware that an AC coalition will make him low man in the triad without much cost to either A or C, and if he cannot have a BC coalition, he probably prefers an AB coalition to none at all.

What should A do in this situation, assuming that he cannot, in the short run, reduce the strength of either B or C enough to make a BC coalition ineffectual? If he can do that, he ought to. But if he cannot, he is well advised to form a coalition with either B or C before they sign up with each other.

Which one does he choose? The AC coalition is tempting. C is more eager to join A than is B, who has his heart set on the BC coalition. C, being weaker than B, will probably move to a more convenient and obliging coalition partner. Moreover, since B presents the greater threat to A's authority, it may seem imprudent to strengthen him further by an AB coalition. Nevertheless, in nine cases out of ten, the right choice for the manager who finds himself in a hierarchical triad is to form the AB coalition if he can. It is the only coalition that does not undermine the table of organization or interfere with the organization's program, and the manager ought to prefer it as a matter of principle. But even on the basis of expediency, he is more likely to gain than to lose by upholding the authority of his principal subordinate.

The AC coalition, sometimes called an improper coalition, preserves A's authority at the cost of creating an ambiguous relationship between B and C. B continues to claim authority over C as an individual but is dominated by the AC coalition, in which C is a partner. Under this arrangement, neither B nor C can exercise authority with any confidence, and the organizational program for which the triad is responsible is likely to suffer accordingly.

Crisis management

If the new manager does not establish his authority early, the chance of his doing it later is exceedingly thin. Conversely, once authority is established, it tends to persist as long as the incumbent takes his work seriously and continues in good health *if* he is able to cope with crises as they arise. Regardless of how long and well he has handled his routine responsibilities, nearly every manager must sometimes confront a major crisis that puts his continuation in question.

Some people's routines, as Everett Hughes has remarked, consist of dealing with other people's emergencies. An organization that handles emergencies routinely does not define them as crises. A fire is not a crisis for a fire department; putting out fires is its routine responsibility. Any fire is a crisis for a school, however, and if an alarm is sent out for a school fire and the firemen fail to respond because of an equipment breakdown, that is a crisis for the fire department.

An organizational crisis may be defined as a problem that calls for maximum effort. The manager's role in eliciting this maximum effort is both symbolic and practical. Symbolically, he personifies the organization's determination to resolve the problem and provides a model of energy and devotion for other members to imitate. Practically, he is responsible for setting up the temporary social structure that every real crisis requires and for overseeing it until the crisis has passed.

Time being always of the essence in crisis, it is convenient—although a little artificial—to describe the manager's responses as a sequence of seven stages:

1. recognition of the crisis
2. appearance on the scene
3. recruitment of a crisis council
4. mobilization of resources
5. enactment of a plan
6. announcement of the outcome
7. distribution of rewards.

The manager's recognition of a crisis in his organization should be dramatic, instantaneous, and unmistakable. When the news arrives in the middle of the night, it is seldom advisable to wait until morning to react. There is very little danger in wrongly identifying a noncrisis as a crisis; it will give everyone concerned an interlude of pleasurable excitement and probably be remembered as a crisis surmounted. There is always a grave danger of responding too slowly or too feebly to a crisis announcement. By morning the situation may be irretrievable.

As soon as a crisis has been recognized, the manager must get to its scene, even if the crisis is inconveniently located or he has better facilities for working on it somewhere else. Any long delay in appearing on the scene is likely to destroy his authority, regardless of the eventual outcome of the crisis. I have known the manager of an international enterprise to lose control of it because when one of his subordinate managers was missing at sea in a disabled company boat, he directed rescue operations from the home office instead of going to the port from which the search was being conducted. The search was successful, but the stay-at-home manager never recovered his authority in that part of the world. The implication in that case was one of neglectfulness. In other instances, the manager's absence from the scene convicts him of timidity or cowardice. The college president who does not come out of his office to face a student riot but sends a dean in his place might as well resign then and there instead of waiting to discover that his usefulness is ended.

Once on the scene, the manager often finds himself in the peculiar position of having to sustain a mood of urgency without doing very much. The obvious organizational responses—putting in the fire alarm, closing the driveway to traffic, getting the cash out of the safe, finding the night watchman—are likely to have been done already. The less obvious steps that will need to be taken require more information and advice than are yet available. It is at this point that the manager finds himself recruiting an ad hoc council who will stay by his side until the crisis is over. He is free to name anyone in the organization to that council, but in most instances there are certain people who must be included if the council is to have quick and frictionless access to the organization's facilities. In a very small organization, the crisis council may have only two or three members, while the council assembled by President Kennedy for the Cuban missile crisis included about fifty officials of varying rank and function who spent nearly twenty-four hours a day for more than two weeks working together in the White House in close contact with the President until the crisis was

over.[19] A crisis council is almost invariably more democratic than
the table of organization from which its members are drawn. In
the ideal case, the members treat each other as equals in the development of information, advice, and alternative contingency plans
for the manager's consideration. When the opinion of the council
on any point is unanimous, it prevails; when there is a division of
opinion in the council, the manager is free to follow the advice of
either the majority or minority without anticipating resistance.

One of the first recommendations of a crisis council is likely to
be some sort of mobilization whereby the entire organization is
alerted to the seriousness of the crisis, and all sorts of people and
facilities are made ready to be used in contingencies that will
probably not occur. This move, too, has both symbolic and practical purposes. Symbolically, it announces the fateful character of
the organization's struggle for survival and the temporary suspen-
sion of other organizational goals. Practically, it enlarges the
manager's ability to respond to unforeseen events and to deploy
the resources of the organization in new combinations.

The next stage in the management of the crisis is the enactment of a plan. What that plan will be about depends, of course,
on the nature of the crisis, which may be a battle or an election, a
championship game or a corporate takeover, a budget hearing or a
hurricane, a strike or a schism. The common principles that apply
to these diverse events are few but important. First, any plan is
better than moment-to-moment improvisation. Second, once a plan
has been adopted, all the weight of the organization should be
thrown behind it. Third, every plan for a crisis should include
provision for the worst possible outcome. It ought to take for
granted Murphy's law ("Whatever can go wrong, will") and include some provision for each of Murphy's contingencies.

Terminating a crisis neatly, once the danger has passed, is
nearly as important as recognizing it at the beginning. This is the
step most often scanted. Flushed by success and exhausted by their
efforts, the members of the crisis council return to their normal
duties, leaving their organizational audience in confusion. (The
reserve units called up during the Cuban missile crisis were not
sent home until many months later.) A better procedure is to wind
the crisis up emphatically by announcing its termination, dissolving
the crisis council, demobilizing the reserves, evaluating the out-

come, and distributing rewards or thanks to those who served and those who only stood and waited.

None of the foregoing advice is meant to obscure or contradict the suggestion made in the previous chapter that the good manager ought to have relatively few organizational crises and ought to prepare for them long in advance. Nevertheless, it is probably impossible in most types of organization for a manager to establish his authority securely until he has surmounted at least one major crisis. It is only then that he may dare to think of his authority as secure.

How to recognize secure authority

The marks of firmly established authority differ somewhat from one type of organization to another and according to managerial styles, but there are certain neat little clues which seem to identify a firmly seated manager under nearly all conditions:

1. His subordinates come to him for advice and instruction; he seldom has to send for them on routine matters.

2. He is able to make suggestions to subordinates that are neither ignored nor misconstrued as orders.

3. He can go anywhere in the organization without experiencing embarrassment or constraint.

4. His closest working associates are those who are closest to him in formal authority.

5. Gossip about the private lives of people in the organization seldom reaches him, but he is almost the first to hear about a new organizational problem.

6. The matters referred to him for decision are, for the most part, those he wants referred. Subordinates do not hesitate to make other decisions on their own.

7. When he returns to the organization after an absence, he does not expect to be confronted with a crisis.

8. His subordinates have sharp differences over organizational policies, which do not seem to lead to personal quarrels.

9. The rank-and-file members of the organization seem genuinely pleased when they run into him unexpectedly.

10. When he presides at a meeting of subordinates, there is never any problem of stimulating discussion. On the other hand, he is usually able to suspend the discussion of a controversial topic and go on to something else.

11. When he attends a meeting presided over by one of his subordinates, it seems to run quite normally.

12. There is no one in the organization that he has to consult about promotions, appointments, or expenditures except those persons he is supposed to consult under the table of organization.

13. Within wide limits, he can adjust his personal workload upward or downward without adversely affecting the organizational program.

14. There is less turnover and absenteeism among his close associates than elsewhere in the organization. When places close to him fall vacant, there is considerable competition for them.

15. He never has to confront a rebellious coalition and never joins an improper coalition.

2:Communication

The Guv'nor addresses:

> *Co-Director Michael Yates as* Mike
> *Assistant Director Michael Yates as* Michael
> *Sectional Manager Michael Yates as* Mr. Yates
> *Sectional Assistant Michael Yates as* Yates
> *Apprentice Michael Yates as* Michael
> *Night-watchman Michael Yates as* Mike

STEPHEN POTTER

Communication and consensus

The manager's task of holding the organization together requires an adequate flow of information upward and downward, and inward and outward. The adequacy of this information flow is measured by the consensus that results from it; that is, the extent to which members of the organization come to agree about the organization's goals.

With high consensus, an organization will have few quarrels; with intermediate consensus, there will be many quarrels, but most of them will be resolved or contained; with low consensus, there will be frequent and severe conflicts and any one of them may lead to a crisis.

Communication and consensus are intimately related, but the relationship is too complex to be reduced to a simple formula. On the one hand, the improvement of consensus ordinarily requires

49

increased communication. On the other hand, an increase in the flow of information between two parts of an organization can undermine an existing consensus.

Every organization can be analyzed as a communication network, as Chester Barnard showed long ago in a book called *The Functions of the Executive*.[1] Networks of this kind are fascinating. They come in all sorts of shapes—pyramidal, serial, circular, and radial, for example—and in all sizes, and they use a variety of devices to code and transmit information. The analysis of the multiple factors that affect the efficiency of a communication network —such as physical distance, social distance, commonality of language, extraneous noise, authentication, and circuit design—is perennially interesting.

The practical problems of communication that every active manager must face present themselves in simpler form. The significant questions for him look something like this:

1. How can the routine reports I receive about the organization's activities be made more reliable, accurate, and comprehensive?

2. With whom should I consult before making decisions? Who should I inform about decisions after they are made?

3. What information do I need to keep secret? How?

4. How much attention should I give to rumormongers and talebearers? What use, if any, should I make of spies?

5. How should I go about repairing or replacing parts of the communications network that have broken down?

6. How can I make my nonverbal communications to the organizational audience mean what I want them to mean?

In actual experience, these six questions and their answers are inextricably entwined, but for purposes of discussion it is convenient to consider them separately.

Routine reports

The easiest way to make one's mark as a manager is to improve the quality of the routine reports the organization produces—hourly, daily, weekly, monthly, quarterly, annually; in written, graphic, or numerical form—about its ongoing activities. This is often quite easy to do, because there are very few people who grasp the importance of routine reporting and even fewer who understand how to set up appropriate reporting procedures. Systems of routine reporting deteriorate in use, so that even the best system needs to be reviewed and reformed periodically.

The first step for a manager in setting up or reforming a system of routine reports is to determine his own priorities. Top-priority reports will claim his attention as fast and as often as they appear. Middle-priority reports are needed for occasional reference. Low-priority reports refer to matters that do not interest him much.

A good deal of care, and as much expense as necessary, ought to be lavished on the production of top-priority reports. It goes without saying that reports in this category should be as prompt, accurate, and complete as is humanly possible, and that they should be in a form that permits comparison with other organizations, with past performance, and with projected achievements.

As usual, it may be helpful to visualize a concrete case. Let us consider a public high school, for the sake of illustration.

The most important routine report that comes to the high school principal is the daily attendance report (Table 8), which shows the number of students and teachers present and absent by class and grade, together with the names of absentees and the number of persons who have joined or left the roster since the previous daily report. A well-designed reporting form ought to provide a summary absenteeism rate for the entire school and the corresponding rates for yesterday, last week, and a year ago. If records of lateness are kept, there will be a temptation to add a comparable summary of lateness to the daily attendance report, but unless lateness has some special local significance, the temptation should be resisted. Lateness and absenteeism are both good (negative) indicators of morale, but they are so closely related that only the absenteeism rate need be calculated. For both the producers and the users of a routine report, it is nearly as important to keep superfluous information out as to get essential information in. When computers are used, this is much harder to do, by the way.

Let us suppose that school begins every morning at 8:30. The

Table 8

BRADFORD HIGH SCHOOL

Daily Attendance Report

For: _____   Prepared by: _____
   Day   Date

			TEACHER	ABS	ROSTER	LATE	ABSENT TODAY	ABSENT YESTERDAY
Grade 9	Class	9a	Brady	( )	____	____	____	____
		9b	Perrotti	( )	____	____	____	____
		9c	Martinez	( )	____	____	____	____
		9d	Smith	( )	____	____	____	____
Grade 10	Class	10a	Emlig	( )	____	____	____	____
		10b	Crawford	( )	____	____	____	____
		10c	Moody	( )	____	____	____	____
Grade 11	Class	11a	Levy	( )	____	____	____	____
		11b	Laliberte	( )	____	____	____	____
		11c	Gross	( )	____	____	____	____
Grade 12	Class	12a	Frisch	( )	____	____	____	____
		12b	Zyler	( )	____	____	____	____
		12c	Muzzy	( )	____	____	____	____
Ungraded Class			Harth	( )	____	____	____	____
			SCHOOL TOTALS	____	____	____	____	____

CUMULATIVE ABSENCES TO THIS DATE _____

DITTO THIS DAY LAST YEAR _____

% ABSENT   TODAY _____

           YESTERDAY _____

           THIS DAY LAST WEEK _____

           THIS DAY LAST YEAR _____

           ADDITIONS TO ROSTER _____

           SUBTRACTIONS FROM ROSTER _____

daily attendance report, preferably on a single sheet of paper, ought to be available by 9:30. Like nearly all top-priority reports, it has multiple functions. If the report is usually on time and complete, the principal is likely to take its accuracy for granted after a while. He ought not to do so since, in the first place, reports of human behavior are inherently fallible and, in the second place, systems of routine reporting tend to deteriorate. The principal must remind himself to verify the information in the daily attendance report from time to time and to raise a terrible fuss whenever he finds an error. The enumeration of absentees can be verified by going to a classroom and comparing the number of students physically present with the number listed as present. The total number present and absent in a given category can be compared with the number of names on the official roster. The arithmetic of totals and percentages can be verified by calculation. The figures for yesterday or last year may be checked against yesterday's or last year's reports in the files. Nit-picking procedures like these will not only help to keep the report trustworthy, they will also uncover anomalous and irregular situations of which the principal ought to be aware.

Weekly reporting is relatively unimportant in a school; school weeks are of uneven length because of holidays, recesses, examinations, and other special events. Months are more significant. The principal's top-priority reports will certainly include a monthly attendance report; a monthly financial report that tells him where he is running ahead of or behind the budget; a utilities report summarizing the school's consumption of electricity, fuel oil, telephone service, etc., and comparing current consumption with past and anticipated consumption; and an inventory report, showing supplies on hand, with a summary of recent deliveries and issues. Unless this last report is carefully made, and just as carefully verified, considerable pilferage is likely to occur. The principal may well feel that his attention ought to be given to more profound educational issues, but unless he is willing to endure the demoralization that accompanies widespread wastage and pilferage, he had better give the utilities and inventory reports his full attention when they come to him.

The other significant reporting periods for a high school are the school term and the school year. Some reports are prepared both for the term and for the year, and others for the year only. Just as the daily report generates a monthly report, so each monthly report generates a term or annual report. Nonetheless, there are some important reports that are solely annual; for example, an academic achievement report, which shows the average grades assigned to students by level and subject, the average scores obtained by the school's students on standard achievement tests like the college entrance examinations, the ratio of successful grade completions to the entering population of each grade, and the number of college applications and acceptances for the graduating class. This report, although complicated in appearance, is simple in substance and absolutely essential; without it, the school is flying blind.

We have lingered a long time in the high school principal's office in order to show how numerous and diverse are the minimum elements of information he needs to do his job in a rational way. Most high schools do not have as good a system of routine reporting as the one outlined above. Instead, the principal receives a great volume of middle- and low-priority information that ought to stop lower down in the organization or not be gathered at all. Even a superficial analysis of the flow of paper in most high schools—and other organizations—will show people filling out forms in quintuplicate when one copy would be amply sufficient, keeping elaborate records for no purpose, obtaining redundant approval for routine actions, or preparing periodic reports that no one ever sees. It is only by pruning the overgrowth of red tape that the flowers of useful information can be made to grow.

In another type of organization, the routine reports that come to a manager might be more analytical and less descriptive. For example, an old study of the organizational performance of insurance agencies by Seashore and Yuchtman at the University of Michigan refers to such variables reported to agency managers as production costs per thousand dollars of insurance carried, maintenance costs per hundred dollars of premium collected, number of lives covered per one thousand insurables in the population, and so on for a total of seventy-six numerical indicators.[2] Curiously, however, the total volume of information required for effective management does not seem to vary in proportion to the size or complexity of the organization, if only because the ability of a single mind to absorb and remember information is limited. The larger the organization, the more severely must information be sifted and screened before it reaches the top. What happens then is pretty much the same in all well-run organizations: the report is scanned and its main outlines are remembered; occasionally some item in it stimulates further action.

When and whom to consult

One of the most common types of managerial error is the failure to consult someone who is entitled to be consulted about a particular matter. Just as it is said to be impossible to finish a sailboat race without making at least a few errors of judgment, so it is probably impossible to manage an organization without making some errors in consultation, but success usually goes to the skipper with the fewest errors.

The reason proper consultation is so hard to achieve is that it involves actions that run counter to the normal impulses of a good manager. Consultation interposes delays between the formulation and the execution of a project, elicits foolish and irrelevant objections, and leads to modifications that tarnish the original luster of the thing. Consultation with subordinates often *feels* uncomfortable. The manager has the feeling of going hat in hand to beg or buy the support he could as easily command. But nine times out of ten he will do better to suffer the discomfort of full consultation than to omit any part of it.

The most essential persons to be consulted in advance of a managerial decision are the subordinate managers and staff advisers who will have to carry it out. The desirability of consulting those who are directly affected is self-evident: they are likely to have vital information about whether and how the decision can be implemented. The manager who doesn't get that information in advance is likely to make a fool of himself whenever he issues a directive, like the engineering executives in the machine shop studied by Donald Roy who periodically introduced new procedures that crippled production until the workmen evolved methods of circumventing them.[3]

But getting advice is only one of the twin purposes of consultation. The other and equally important purpose is to elicit consent. People are much more likely to support a decision they helped to make, or think they helped to make, than the same decision imposed on them from above. This magic is so powerful that even a nominal or illusory participation in the making of a decision is often sufficient to secure the support of those who would otherwise oppose it.

It is possible to devise Machiavellian tricks that make use of this effect, for example, by putting obvious mistakes and defects into a proposal so that everyone consulted will find it easy to make suggestions for improvement and to ascertain later that their suggestions have been followed. Even without such conniving, when the opponents of a project are seriously consulted and induced to participate in the planning stage, they often are irresistibly drawn toward the project despite their initial opposition.

Like most magic spells, this one can turn upon its user. The manager who seeks advice need not take it, but he must never seem to despise it. Hell hath no fury like a consultant scorned.

To consult all the subordinate managers and staff advisers directly affected by a prospective decision is hardly more than ordinary prudence. Consultation with those who may be indirectly affected is a more delicate operation and calls for more insight into organizational processes. This sort of consultation always runs the risk of arousing opposition in quarters where neither support or opposition were called for. Nevertheless, because the indirect effects of decisions are so significant—as when the decision to expand one department of an organization is perceived as a hostile act by departments not expanded—the need for advice and consent often extends far beyond that part of an organization which seems to be directly concerned. A skillful manager will extend the consultation process as far as he can without creating needless problems, which is generally a good bit further than his natural inclination would take him.

It goes without saying that the rank-and-file members of an organization ought to be consulted also. But except in organizational crises, as previously described, a manager ought not to go around his subordinate managers to reach the rank and file. Depending upon the organizational structure, he has the choice of encouraging subordinate managers to consult in their turn, or of organizing consultative sessions that include everyone. Whether he deals with the rank and file en masse or with their designated representatives, it is seldom useful for him to consult them without involving subordinate managers in one way or another. As to his personal assistants, the less the manager depends on their advice in making decisions, the better. If he cannot do it without them, he ought at least take care to conceal whatever influence they have.

There are several special types of consultation that call for some modification of the foregoing principles. Among these are consultation with committees, grievance procedures, and consultation with outside experts.

CONSULTATION WITH COMMITTEES

The great comic theorist of modern organizations, Professor Parkinson, once suggested a formal study of this subject to be known as commitology, and mentioned in passing the interesting fact that the word *committee* was originally singular and denoted a person appointed to represent the legal interests of a lunatic. The phenomenon is much older and wider than the word, however. Every organization, even a street-corner gang, seems to generate some committees. Some large organizations have thousands of committees, with all sorts of administrative, judicial, and technical functions. We will confine our attention here to committees designed primarily for consultation. Within this category, there are standing committees, special committees, and ad hoc committees.

The universal annoyance with committees is partly explained by the fact that many or most committee meetings are occupied with business that is of little interest to many or most of the participants. But from the standpoint of a manager, no meeting of a committee within his jurisdiction is really dull. The committee is an instrument that serves his interests much more than the interests of other members, no matter how democratic and egalitarian its proceedings may be.

Although commitology is not likely to become a recognized social science, there have been several excellent and careful studies of how committees operate and what factors influence them—for example, the laboratory studies of Harold Guetzkow[4] and of James David Barber,[5] and the observational studies of Richard F. Fenno, Jr.,[6] and of Leonard Berkowitz.[7] The findings of these studies, taken together, suggest that committees with organizational tasks work best under a strong chairman who poses many questions, speaks more to the whole group than to individuals, defines the issues, proposes solutions, keeps the discussion on its track, relates the amount of discussion to the available time, and attempts to reach and summarize group decisions. "There is a general expectation," writes Berkowitz in summarizing his study of seventy-two committees in business, industry, and government, "that the socially designated leader, the chairman, should be the sole major behavioral leader." He goes on to say that the sharing of leadership by other members seems to leave the members of a committee dissatisfied with each other and with their deliberations, regardless of whether the committee members who share leadership with the chairman are his supporters or his opponents. The empirical studies also seem to agree that successful chairmen do not attempt to prevent the expression of opposing viewpoints or to force a consensus prematurely. Several studies show that strong chairmen are better liked by their committees than passive chairmen, but also show that chairmen who are outranked by the members of their committees are likely to be passive.

These research results stand in apparent contradiction to what is sometimes called "sensitivity training," a method whereby people in large organizations are taught sensitivity in human relations as a means of developing "interpersonal competence." The formula for a successful sensitivity training group is nearly the opposite of the formula for a successful committee. The training group works best with a passive, permissive leader who makes no attempt to hold discussions to a fixed agenda or a definite time schedule, but rather encourages digressions that reveal the hidden emotions of the participants to each other and ultimately to themselves. This approach makes sense in its own context, which is closely related to group therapy, and the people who are sent by large organizations to participate in such training—for example, the government officials who attend the Federal Executive Institute in Charlottesville, Virginia—usually find the experience pleasant and educational. But those enthusiasts who attempt to impose the style of the training group on working committees in large organizations sow confusion.

How to Appoint Committees   A *standing committee* is a body with a continuous responsibility that calls for collective rather than individual judgment—for example, the rules committee of a legislative body, the admissions committee of a professional school, the loan committee of a bank. As a rule of thumb, a standing committee should have a minimum of five members and a maximum of perhaps nine, although, of course, there are justifiable exceptions. The reason for the minimum of five is that it implies a working majority of three, which represents about as narrow a spread of collective judgment as can suffice in a situation that calls for collective judgment. The maximum of nine is a less rigid limit, but since most standing committees must meet regularly without the stimulus of an emergency, the difficulty of scheduling meetings for a larger number of people suggests an upper limit in this neighborhood unless the business of the committee is so overwhelmingly important that none of its members is likely to develop conflicting obligations.

The manager of an organization ought never to appoint himself as chairman of a standing committee. By doing so, he defeats the purposes of the standing committee, which are to relieve him of administrative burdens and to substitute a collective judgment for his individual judgment in certain recurrent, noncritical situations. It is usually a good idea, however, for him to be an ex officio member of any standing committee within his jurisdiction so as to have informal access to its meetings and records when matters in which he is especially interested are considered.

The chairman of a standing committee ought to be senior to most of the other members, if only because he has to allocate work to them from time to time. He (or as ever, she) ought not to be a person of extreme opinions with respect to the standing committee's area of interest, or someone new to the organization who does not understand its informal norms. The membership of a standing committee should be as broadly representative as its size permits, with regard to organizational rank, personal characteristics, and factional affiliations.

A *special committee* is typically appointed to consider some knotty problem that the manager cannot resolve through his ordinary pattern of consultation because it is too complex, or too controversial, or too important to be handled in the regular way. Special committees are also appointed on occasion to defer or avoid an otherwise pressing decision, to deflect the onus of an unpopular decision, or to allay suspicions that have arisen in connection with a particular issue. A few special committees are appointed to cope with problems that are intrinsically unimportant but have acquired symbolic significance.

The membership of a special committee ought to be large enough to include all relevant shades of opinion and every important faction of the organization; the only upper limit is the capacity of the organization's largest conference table. A membership of twenty or twenty-five is not excessive. The best chairman for such a committee is a subordinate manager of considerable seniority, preferably with white hair and a good command of parliamentary procedure. The manager who appoints a special committee ought not to make himself a member of it, and unless he has some extraordinary announcement to make, ought never to appear at its meetings or contribute to its deliberations once they have begun. He should, however, start the special committee off with an unequivocal charge, describing its task with as much detail as necessary and indicating clearly what sort of report the committee is supposed to produce, within what interval of time, with what resources, and under what conditions of publicity or secrecy. It is permissible, and even conventional, for a manager to provide him-

Table 9: Rules of thumb for consulted committees

Type of committee	Size of committee	Qualifications of chairman	Manager's participation
Standing	5–9	senior to most other members	as ex officio member
Special	10–30	senior to all other members	through informants
Ad hoc	2–5	interested in assignment	none

self with informal access to the deliberations of a special committee by putting an assistant or a personal friend on it.

An *ad hoc committee* is ordinarily appointed for some noncontroversial, nonrecurrent task such as drafting a statement or inspecting an item offered for sale. A surprising proportion of ad hoc committees have three members; some have only two; five is about the practical maximum. It is important that the members of an ad hoc committee be compatible with each other and competent with respect to the committee's assignment. They do not need to be representative of the organization in any other way and it does not much matter which of them is named as chairman.

Conducting Committee Business   The manager who chairs a standing committee of his own organization is well advised to adopt a style that is simultaneously autocratic and permissive— autocratic with respect to controlling the agenda and determining the scope of the committee's responsibility for each agenda item, permissive in encouraging the free expression of opinions and in allowing room and time for a genuine consensus to develop, even if this means, as it frequently does, that decisions must be deferred from one meeting to the next and then possibly delayed again. A smooth-running committee of this kind may or may not vote formally on the matters before it, but virtually all of its decisions will be unanimous if only because the chairman insists on continuing the discussion of every matter until a sense of unanimity prevails.

The manager's relationship to committees he appoints but does not chair is somewhat different. He is always well advised to adopt an attitude of deference toward such committees and to avoid the slightest appearance of interfering with their deliberations, since any action that they construe as interference is certain to be resented. For this reason, it is essential that when a manager appoints a committee he does not chair he retain a veto, either by stipulating in advance that the committee's decisions will be submitted to him as recommendations, or that they will not take effect until he has reviewed and approved them. This veto must be exercised from time to time even if the manager has no real objection to any of the committee's decisions, or the veto power will atrophy so rapidly that when eventually wanted it may be challenged.

The rule of noninterference with the deliberations of a committee does not prevent the manager's attendance at meetings of a standing committee in his role as an ex officio member, provided he keeps his mouth firmly shut except in response to direct questions. He should not attend the meetings of a special committee except under extraordinary circumstances.

In large organizations, the management of special committees is especially challenging. A special committee is normally appointed to resolve a problem that is complex and controversial. The resolution of such a problem usually has two stages: first, the development of a compromise that is acceptable to all or nearly all the members of the special committee; second, the acceptance of the compromise by the rest of the organization. A special committee that submits a majority report supported by only a bare majority must be regarded as a failure, and, except in extraordinary circumstances, its report ought to be filed and forgotten. A committee that submits unanimous or nearly unanimous recommendations can be rated as successful, but it does not follow that its recommendations should be accepted forthwith. If, by accident or intent, the special committee did not include representatives of all the influential factions involved in the controversy, an acceptable compromise still remains to be achieved. If the special committee did include spokesmen for opposed viewpoints, the production of a unanimous or nearly unanimous report ordinarily signifies that prolonged exposure to the facts of the situation and to each other's arguments, together with some process of conciliation or negotiation, has brought the factions within the special committee into agreement. The chances are, however, that in moving toward a common center, they have lost touch with the constituencies whose viewpoints they were originally chosen to represent. The question of whether these constituencies will accept the compromise reached by their delegates has to be answered before the manager decides whether to implement, reject, or modify the committee's recommendation. For this question to be properly answered, the committee's report should be widely circulated within the organization and nothing else ought be done about it for a while even though the problem is relatively urgent. When action is finally taken on the special committee's recommendation, it must be on the manager's responsibility and not the committee's. The best way to make this plain when acting on a committee's recommendations is to modify them in some respects.

GRIEVANCE PROCEDURES

The hearing of grievances is another specialized type of managerial consultation. In many organizations, the grievance procedure is virtually the only channel through which the manager obtains information about morale, motivation, and conflict at lower levels of the organization. The settlement of grievances can be highly rewarding for both the manager and the organization, but it is intrinsically difficult and requires much more than simple goodwill on the part of a responsible manager.

A grievance is a complaint directed toward an organizational superior with a request for redress. All organizations are full of complaints openly expressed to peers and sometimes to outsiders, but relatively few of them turn into grievances by being attached to a request for redress.

The nondirective interviews that were part of the famous Western Electric study recorded eighty thousand complaints from workers in one industrial plant during a single year and classified them neatly into objectively verifiable complaints, subjective complaints, and nonlogical complaints. The Western Electric investigators concluded that: (1) the underlying attitude of the complainant toward his work and his associates was often more significant in accounting for a complaint than the particular condition that he complained of; (2) the mere opportunity to complain to a receptive listener connected with management had a favorable effect on morale; (3) after telling their complaints to the interviewer, workers often perceived an improvement in the condition complained about even though no objective change had occurred.[8] These effects have been confirmed in subsequent studies and used in organizational counseling programs. A particularly interesting factory study carried out in England by A. J. M. Sykes[9] showed that long-standing grievances held by workers against their foremen could be dissolved by a patterned system of eliciting and discussing complaints without changing the behavior of the foremen in any way.

The differences between such sociopsychological games and a genuine grievance procedure is that the latter, while still providing benefits that seem to follow from the mere airing of complaints, also makes arrangements for management to do something about verifiable grievances and to attend to the real dissatisfactions that underlie many imaginary grievances.

How many of an organization's circulating complaints turn into active grievances depends upon the volume and intensity of complaining, the receptivity of management to grievances, its reputation for fairness, the attitudes of particular managers, and the presence or absence of third parties. A high grievance rate is always a bad sign, but an abnormally low grievance rate is almost equally suspicious. Rensis Likert, in his *New Patterns of Management*, presented statistical evidence to show that industrial workers who are hostile to the enterprise in which they work seldom submit grievances. The same study also showed that people at each level of management overestimate the extent to which their subordinates feel free to express grievances, giving themselves much higher marks for accessibility than they deserve, while rating their own superiors much lower than themselves in this respect.[10]

Well-run organizations have only a small number of grievances, and management reacts to them promptly and vigorously. Most of these grievances fall into a few simple categories that are part of every manager's experience. The most common grounds for grievances are quarrels between superiors and subordinates, discrimination against an individual or a group, breaches of the organization's rules, and neglect of some organizational function.

To handle grievances, the manager may establish an open-door policy whereby anyone in the organization can approach him with a grievance at any time, or he may delegate an ombudsman to hear grievances on his behalf, or authorize a walking delegate to bring him grievances on behalf of the rank and file, or turn over all grievances to an internal tribunal. Some managers follow a closed-door policy, whereby grievances are referred back to lower levels of the organization or simply ignored. This latter policy, although widely practiced, represents the abdication rather than the exercise of managerial responsibility. The other grievance policies invite closer attention.

The open-door policy has a good deal of rhetorical appeal and is often proudly announced by managers who would not dream of following it. Except in very small organizations, it is not an effective way to handle grievances, because the manager does not have enough time to look into the facts of each case, talk to all the people involved, and arrive at a judicious solution. Moreover, an open-door policy favors the least deserving complainants. The neurotic and self-absorbed persons found in every organization will not hesitate to claim the manager's ear, while the more serious people will hesitate to push themselves on him. The manager who tries to follow an open-door policy may come to practice what Max Weber called "cadi justice," the quick and arbitrary disposition of cases by the local tyrant before an admiring audience at the city gates. It is a hazardous role for any manager who lacks the cadi's powers over life and death.

There are two variations of the open-door policy that make it more workable. In one procedure, the open door is only ceremonial. The manager receives every complainant personally but refers him as quickly as possible to an assistant who handles the matter from then on. This procedure is fairly advantageous for complainants but not very advantageous for the manager. The situation is so structured that those who obtain satisfaction are grateful to the assistant while those who do not blame the manager.

A better variation of the open-door policy is practiced by many self-confident managers who, as soon as they understand the nature of the grievance, insist on bringing in the person or persons complained about and conducting all further discussion in this conference of adversaries. This procedure, however, is unfair when persons high in the organization are in the position to take reprisals against lower-ranking parties who offend them at such a conference.

In some organizations, a complainant must go to each intervening level of authority with his grievance before he approaches the open door at the top. This looks superficially reasonable but is so drastically unfair in practice that it must be regarded as a way of repressing rather than handling grievances. It involves excessive wear and tear on the complainant as well as the automatic creation of a coalition of his superiors against him.

The principal alternative to the open-door policy is a system of representation whereby the complainant, the manager, or both are represented by competent agents during the hearing of a grievance. For example, the manager's responsibility for hearing and redressing grievances may be delegated to a committee of subordinates who are placed partly outside of his control in order to assure their impartiality. From the standpoint of management, this is a nearly ideal system; such independent tribunals appear under every civilized form of government. In some types of organization, however, managerial influence is so pervasive that it is very difficult to assemble an impartial tribunal. Despite centuries of experience, military and naval courts-martial are not renowned for impartial justice. In other types of organization, such as industrial corporations, the rank and file do not have enough confidence in management to submit their grievances to a managerially appointed tribunal. The recourse in such cases is an arbitration board composed of outsiders or including rank-and-file representatives.

Ombudsmen have recently been installed in many American organizations. The ombudsman is an autonomous representative of management assigned to hear complaints, identify justifiable grievances, and press for redress on behalf of the complainant and others in the same situation. In the Scandinavian governments, which originated this office, the ombudsman relies only on public opinion and his powers of persuasion to get grievances redressed. A few American bureaucracies that have ombudsmen (for example, a number of state prisons) empower them to redress certain grievances on their own authority. Under either arrangement, the ombudsman acts as a broker between the management that appoints him and the clients whose interests he is supposed to protect. The role is necessarily uncomfortable, and he must be effectively insulated from the rest of the organization in order to function.

Organizations of similar type often develop quite dissimilar modes of handling grievances that seem nevertheless to work about equally well, as illustrated by Steven A. Richardson's comparative study of grievance procedures on British and American merchant ships. When a British sailor has a complaint, his first step is to enlist the sympathy and support of his fellow sailors, who, as a delegation, take the complaint first to the bosun, then to the mate, and then, if it is still unsettled, to the captain. On American ships, the elected union delegate takes charge of all grievances and settles most of them by direct negotiation with the bosun, who is himself a union member. Only under unusual circumstances does the delegate go above the bosun's head to the mate or the captain.[11]

The appointment of a third party to handle grievances does not fully relieve a manager of participation in the process. He will still be involved in the grievances of his immediate subordinates, in appeals from grievance decisions at lower levels, and in the supplemental complaints inevitably generated by a grievance procedure. Whether he handles grievances directly or at second hand, there are certain principles that a responsible manager ought to keep in mind in order to avoid the pitfalls that await him in such matters. To explain why the risk is higher for him than for his subordinates, we need to digress briefly into the theory of organization.

Every living organization has some aura of sanctity in the eyes of its members—even a bridge club or a street-corner gang. Authority exercised in the name of an organization always has a moral component. Members are expected to obey organizational directives not merely because of self-interest or coercion but also because of the goodness of the organization's purposes and the rightness of its activities. Concepts of duty, loyalty, and justice seem to arise spontaneously in all organizations, regardless of the time, place, or culture in which they are set. The responsible manager of an organization is perceived by its members as the custodian of its moral force. He may be corrupt, lazy, incompetent, or careless without violating this ritual role, but he cannot appear unjust.

Since subordinates lack the monarchical aura, an act of injustice by a subordinate is not likely to disturb the organization nearly as much. On the other hand, the power of an organization to shape the behavior of its members is always dependent on an exchange of benefits between organizational levels. The obedience that members of organizations give to their superiors is given in direct exchange for their superiority over their own subordinates and for the equality they enjoy with their peers. When one side of this exchange is reduced, the other must decline correspondingly. Thus, the manager who undermines the legitimate authority of his subordinates, or fails to defend them against the encroachment of their peers, weakens his own hold on them as well as the organization's capability to carry out its program.

Most of the serious grievances that reach the top of an organization are serious precisely because they involve some dilemma between doing justice and maintaining authority. The janitor foreman fires a man for insubordination; the dismissed janitor admits that he often talked back, but points out that he never refused to do what he was told. The new choirmaster chooses a pretty young soprano as soloist for the Christmas program; she has a smaller vocal range than the older woman who has sung the part for the past five years. The tool-crib boss is demoted for failing to report an increase in pilferage; he claims that he made oral reports, which were disregarded, to the superintendent; the superintendent denies it. The crib man's story is supported by one witness, a machinist who is also his next-door neighbor.

Some grievances, of course, are much more intricate than these examples, but almost all of them involve a managerial dilemma. I remember the case of a small consulting firm that paid high salaries and provided extensive fringe benefits to its employees. It had a low turnover rate and every sign of high morale even though the owner-manager traveled extensively in the conduct of the business and was often out of the office and out of the country for long periods of time. One day he hit upon the idea of rewarding his employees with a profit-sharing plan. When the plan was finally drawn up, approved by the tax authorities, and put into effect, he was startled to experience a sharp decline in his rapport with subordinates; but it was only much later, when a delegation came to him with a formal complaint, that he grasped the problem. As soon as the employees acquired an interest in profitability, they looked about for ways of keeping costs down. This reaction, of course, is one of the objectives of a profit-sharing plan. In this particular enterprise, there were relatively few costs that could be reduced by employee initiative. The largest variable category was the owner-manager's expense for travel and entertainment in dealings with clients. The delegation came to complain about the loss of profits chargeable to his customary style of doing business, and demanded, among other things, that he cease to travel first class and begin to patronize cheaper restaurants. The grievance was eventually resolved, but not without permanent damage to the organization.

The rules of prudence for threading one's way through serious grievances are remarkably simple.

The first rule is to listen carefully to the original complaint. Never scold the complainant at this stage and never, never appear to take his side. Then, as quickly as possible, listen to the person or persons complained about. Watch as well as listen; gestures and facial expressions are significant. Then go yourself—do not send someone else—to look at the objective evidence—the scene of the accident, the time cards for the day, the trash dumped out the window. Write down everything you hear and see. Listen to other witnesses, including, as a matter of course, all the people in intervening positions between you and the parties. Keep an open mind and make no commitments to either side until all the evidence is in.

The second rule is to follow the evidence where it leads without considering possible embarrassment to individuals or damage to the organization. This is nearly always a safer course than attempting to hush up a scandal.

The third and harshest rule is to favor a superior over his subordinate when the evidence is insufficient to decide between them. Faced with a conflict of testimony that cannot be resolved objectively, it is generally better to trust the higher-ranking witness than to reject both stories. After a fight so serious that one of the parties must leave the organization, it is usually better to dismiss the subordinate than to expel both parties. The manager may fancy himself as an impartial tribunal, but organizational justice is best served in the long run by protecting organizational authority unless there is clear evidence that it has been abused.

The fourth rule is to force the complainant to propose the remedy for a grievance. Indeed, he should be asked to specify the redress he wants when he makes his original complaint. (A surprising number of real grievances turn out to have no practicable remedy.) When a complaint is found to be justified, the person or persons complained against should be given an opportunity to discuss, revise, and, if possible, agree to the proposed remedy before it is put into effect.

The fifth rule is to treat similar grievances as uniformly as possible, recognizing that uneven justice is no justice at all. This means, among other things, that grievance procedures should not be secret and that any decision about a grievance should be recognized as a possible precedent for the settlement of future grievances of the same kind.

OUTSIDE EXPERTS

Consultation with outside experts is another specialized form of managerial communication. These include technicians engaged for a specific task, such as surveyors or appraisers; professional advisers retained on a semipermanent basis, such as lawyers and accountants; and outsiders who provide such managerial services as market research, supervisor training, or long-range planning.

Most of the purposes for which outside experts are hired are bona fide; their advice is often helpful and sometimes indispensable. But the outside expert is not always brought onto the organizational scene just for his ostensible function.[12]

Outside experts are sometimes called in to decide a controversial issue that cannot be settled internally without hard feelings. In such a case, the fiction that the decision is based on impartial expertise helps to soften the chagrin of the losers. Even when the fiction is not entirely credible, some of the resentment provoked by the decision will be harmlessly deflected toward the outsiders.

A consultant is sometimes brought in not to discover new facts but to force facts already known upon the attention of some reluctant part of the organization. Thus, a survey of morale among the rank and file may be undertaken in order to compel subordinate managers to do something about morale problems already known to exist.

An outside expert may be called in to advise a manager to do something he has already decided to do and to provide justifications for doing it that can be displayed to various audiences inside and outside the organization. Outside experts are also likely to be retained for a number of tasks that are too painful for a manager to undertake in his own name—for example, the auditing of financial records to uncover embezzlement or a reclassification of personnel that modifies the existing pattern of career expectations.

The outsider need not be corrupt to be malleable. The precarious character of a consultant's employment makes him acutely responsive to the client's demands, expressed or unexpressed, while the client is unlikely to select a consultant who does not view his problems in a sympathetic light.

The mere enumeration of these ulterior purposes suggests that consultants should be used very sparingly; they should also be selected, engaged, and actively supervised by the manager to whom they report, discouraged from improvising their own liaisons with other parts of the organization, and replaced at the first intimation that they are participating in the organization's internal intrigues.

An outside consultant is a managerial weapon and should be neither used carelessly nor left unguarded.

AFTER CONSULTATION

If consultation should precede nearly every managerial decision, the diffusion of information ought to follow as a matter of course. The minimum requirement is that everyone consulted about a managerial decision should be fully informed about the decision as soon as it has been made. This principle, although self-evident, is often violated by managers in a hurry or obsessed with secrecy, almost always to their own disadvantage.

The general problem of whom to inform about what is shared by everyone from the top to the bottom of every organization, and nearly all of these people occasionally tell someone what he shouldn't know or fail to tell him what he should know. Errors of the first kind usually have trivial consequences from the organization's standpoint, although they may be serious for individuals. The error of not telling people what they need to know is much more troublesome for the organization because it leads both to inappropriate behavior and hurt feelings. The father of the infant princess who later became the Sleeping Beauty invited all the fairies in his kingdom to the christening feast, but according to the old tale he forgot one important fairy, who became so furious at the slight that she came to the celebration uninvited and canceled out the other fairies' blessings by putting a curse on the child. This sort of thing happens in large organizations every day, when people who are entitled to be informed about some matter are carelessly overlooked.

The manager, as I said before, shares this problem with everyone else; but his failures to diffuse needed information have greater effect, partly because he has more information to diffuse, partly because insults from him, like courtesies from him, carry unusual weight. There is no way to avoid errors of omission completely, but their occurrence can be greatly reduced by constant effort and by using checklists of names.

It is nearly impossible for someone at the top of an organization to understand how little of the organization is visible to people at lower levels. It is not uncommon for employee surveys to turn up employees who cannot correctly identify their own supervisors, the department in which they work, or the nature of the enterprise.

In a study I conducted many years ago, we found that the majority of officers in an air force division were unfamiliar with the mission of their own unit as set down in the organization's manual. The majority of enlisted men could not identify their own jobs and had only an approximate idea of their own duties. Neither junior officers nor enlisted personnel had any clear picture of the division's structure or understood its relationship to the military and civilian organizations with which it had routine contact. The commanding general of the division, an officer famous for his solid achievements and his flamboyant style, found some of these results incredible. "They couldn't not know their own squadron commanders," he objected, "any more than not know me." The next survey of the division's personnel asked them to identify their commanding general; a sizable percentage had never heard his name.

People in organizations must not be expected to acquire a standard inventory of information by osmosis. They need to have it systematically communicated to them by means of orientation sessions, written materials circulated for study, posted signs, public assemblies, newsletters, and other devices. What is meant to be remembered must then be frequently repeated. Internal orientation is an essential, continuous activity in any well-run organization.

Secrecy and security

Every organization has some need for secrecy. Generally speaking, poor managers try to keep secret as much information as possible, while good managers try to have as few secrets as possible.

The attempt to guard a large amount of information is intrinsically self-defeating. A large stock of secrets requires a large number of custodians and the frequent deposit and withdrawal of confidential documents. It is highly unlikely that all the custodians can be trusted or that adequate surveillance can be maintained of the traffic in secret materials. The effort to keep many secrets makes it difficult to protect the few secrets that really matter. In organizations already plagued by excessive secrecy, there is usually some effort made to identify the real secrets by special labels like "Top Secret" or "For Eyes Only," and by ritual devices like burn-bags and coding machines. On balance, these probably make the real secrets more vulnerable by flagging their locations.

Once introduced into an organization, security classification generally spreads like a fungus, for obvious reasons. The right to keep organizational secrets is always a mark of organizational status—symbolically, because it signifies that the organization trusts the keeper; practically, because secret information gives its keeper a tactical advantage in the conduct of his own affairs. Since security classifications are among the cheapest of all status symbols, they are likely to be overproduced. The effects of such overproduction are long-lasting, for the security label attached to trivial or outdated information makes declassification difficult. The United States government, a notable victim of this blight, stores thousands of tons of unimportant documents that, because of their security labels, cannot be easily inspected or thrown away.

Secrecy is costly for an organization in many other ways. It slows down important communications and interferes with routine ones, it creates pockets of ignorance at points where knowledge is needed, and it engenders suspicion and serves to conceal fraud, malfeasance, and sabotage. The availability of a cloak of secrecy always seems to encourage wrongdoing by organizational functionaries. On the one hand, they can justify wrongdoing by the excuse of security. On the other hand, the absence of feedback makes it difficult to distinguish between normal and abnormal conduct.

The manager who takes a secret action ought to ask himself, as Edmond Cahn has suggested, such questions as: How much the public view the action if all the facts, motives, and profits were revealed? How would you characterize the action if it had been done by your worst enemy?[13]

Managerial secrecy ought, ideally, to be restricted to those few items of information whose revelation would damage the organization, but not expose it to any shame. Most items of information that answer this description fall into one of three categories: (1) plans of action that would be hampered or prevented if prematurely revealed, such as battle plans, site acquisition plans, merger plans, and campaign plans; (2) knowledge that is useful to the organization but would be less useful if known to outsiders, such as a product formula or a map showing buried treasure; or (3) information about persons, collected by the organization for proper purposes, which might cause embarrassment or suffering to them if made public, such as performance ratings and disciplinary records.

Some other types of information are kept secret by organizations primarily to entertain or impress their members. The remarkable Seven Society at the University of Virginia is a very old student group known to make donations to college projects and to issue occasional statements on local issues. Everything else about it is secret, with the sole exception that at a member's death the fact of his having belonged to the society is finally made public. Secrecy of this kind is a game played for its own sake. Similar games are played for political, religious, social, and criminal purposes. The manager of a secret society has some unique problems, but they have not been empirically studied and will not be discussed here. Ordinary organizations operate better with minimum secrecy, and the manager who systematically attempts to reduce the number of locked files and confidential stamps in his organization will be amazed to discover how much sensitive and explosive information becomes harmless when exposed to the light of day.

The best methods of keeping a real secret, of course, remain what they have always been. Tell it sparingly and only to people who have an unmistakable need to know. Make the fewest possible documents and conceal them unobtrusively. Trust no strangers.

Spies and rumormongers

The communication network of every organization, large or small, has a seamy underside for the circulation of stolen information and misinformation. Many organizations must remain on guard against spies sent from outside. Nearly every organization has amateur spies who snoop for fun and profit. In nearly all organizations, there is some circulation of false or grossly exaggerated rumors.

On the large scene of public affairs, spying has been practiced throughout history, but for every general or statesman who has known how to make good use of spies, another has been led to ruin by them. Without the blundering of their own spies, the British might have put down the American Revolution. General McClellan could probably have won the Civil War for the Union in 1862 had he not relied upon the reports of Confederate strength obtained for him at great expense by the Pinkertons. The Vietnam disaster could not have begun or been continued by the United States without the maladroit assistance of an army of unreliable spies. Without their secret agents, Mary Queen of Scots might have died in bed, Napoleon might have retained his crown, and President Nixon might have occupied a distinguished place in American history.

The little that is publicly known about industrial and commercial espionage suggests that these forms of spying, too, are often more damaging to their users than to their intended victims.

Aside from the obvious risks—betrayal by double agents, exposure of one's own plans, being lured by the other side into acting on false information—there is the overriding risk that the information provided by spies will be biased in favor of their continued employment. They are thus inclined to suppress information that casts doubt upon their earlier reports or that is inconsistent with the picture of the situation they have built up. This bias often sets the stage for disaster.

Nevertheless, there are some managerial occasions that do call for spying inside or outside the organization; for example, an adversary is known to be deploying a secret weapon and it is essential to have more information about it, or a conspiracy is brewing in the organization and one of the conspirators is willing to reveal it. Note, however, that the first of these problems might be better handled by scouting than by spying, while the second needs a voluntary informant rather than a spy. The secret agent planted somewhere to report regularly may become either an agent provocateur who fabricates conspiracies in order to betray them, or a real conspirator who lulls his employer with false information. The scout sent out from one's own ranks and the voluntary informant who reveals a plot have much more to lose than to gain if their information turns out to be false. A spy who might safely provide false information should never be trusted as far as the door.

GRAPEVINES

It is usually possible for a manager to find out something about how rumors circulate in his organization and, within limits, to adapt the process to the organization's advantage.

A classic experiment, first developed by Gordon Allport, is often staged in psychology classrooms to show how information is distorted in the transmittal of a rumor.[14] A student chosen at random from the class is handed a picture with a number of complicated details—for example, a summer street scene in a large city showing an ice cream vendor surrounded by several children in the foreground, two dogs being walked on leashes nearby, and a firehouse in the background. The first student is asked to whisper a description of the picture to his neighbor who, in turn, whispers as much as he can remember to his neighbor, and so on through fifteen or twenty persons. After each subject has whispered his version, he writes it down so that changes in the form and content of the message can be traced from the beginning to the end of the chain. The changes that occur are startling and ludicrous. The message that emerged at the end of one such chain, based on the picture described above, was: "The picture shows a burning barn. About fifty horses have been led out of the barn. Some of them are running away."

If we look at the intermediate versions, we find that most of the distortion occurred at the beginning of the chain when the firehouse became a fire, the dogs turned into horses, and the ice cream vendor disappeared. Later on, the description assumed the tripartite form characteristic of folk tales; exaggeration took place —*two* horses became *some* horses, which became *many* horses, which became *fifty* horses—and new elements were invented to fill the logical gaps created by previous distortions. The barn, for example, appeared suddenly as a link between "fire" and "horses." Toward the end of the chain, the story was so condensed and simplified that it could be transmitted from person to person without appreciable distortion.

This process of distortion can often be observed in demoralized organizations, but it is not characteristic of normally functioning organizations. Field studies of rumors in armies, political parties, factories, hospitals, and prisons, for example, have found that most of the rumors that circulate in well-integrated organizations carry substantially accurate information, flow through fairly reliable channels, and are subject to multiple cross-checks that discourage distortions. This kind of communication network is often called a grapevine. In a well-integrated organization it is remarkably quick and reliable.

Generally speaking, an effective grapevine ought to be considered as an organizational asset, partly because it supplements formal channels of communications, and partly because it prevents unfounded rumors and other kinds of misinformation.

A grapevine is capable of transmitting a variety of messages on a variety of topics. What it actually transmits during a given period seems to depend on the supply of and demand for particular kinds of information. The grapevine is most active when information is scarce and the demand for it is high; it is least active when the information is plentiful and the demand for it is low. If an organization's future plans are kept secret, there will be many rumors about future plans. If they are widely publicized, there will be few such rumors and perhaps none at all. Some sorts of information, like scandalous gossip, are always in demand and usually in short supply. When information in this category becomes available, the grapevine transmits it far and wide.

But an organization's demand for information of a particular type can be readily satiated by oversupplying related information even though it is not the precise information demanded. In an invasion convoy, the captain of one ship on which I traveled announced over the ship's loudspeakers every bit of interesting information that came to the bridge, such as a submarine search by escort vessels or a change in the weather at the invasion site. Although there were many uncertainties in the impending invasion, the constant bombardment of announcements so satiated the demand for information that, although the unit to which I belonged had a hyperactive grapevine, it circulated no rumors of any kind until we had disembarked from the ship. The only reliable method of silencing a grapevine is to supply it with more information than it wants on topics related to the information being withheld.

Another somewhat devious method of using a grapevine for managerial purposes is to feed information into it at strategic points, for example, by exposing a confidential paper to known rumormongers. The information may be organizationally relevant, but not suitable for official dissemination, as in the case of a merger negotiation that has not yet reached the stage at which an announcement is possible but ought in fairness to be made known within the organization.

How to repair interrupted communications

One of the most common problems encountered by the managers of organizations is the breakdown of communication between two positions that are closely connected in the table of organization and are supposed to interact routinely. The incumbents may have a personal quarrel, may differ about the purposes of a program for which they share responsibility, may be unable to settle a dispute about authority, or may be unwilling to work together for various other reasons. I once knew a manufacturing company that had only two vice-presidents, one for marketing and one for production. Although they worked in the same building, they did not exchange a single word for several years. Like governments that do not recognize each other and have to communicate through neutral embassies, these executives used the president of the company as their intermediary for essential messages.

Communication breakdowns occur at every organizational level and for all sorts of reasons. In the foregoing case, the production vice-president, trained in an advanced branch of engineering, regarded the marketing vice-president as a charlatan bent on degrading the company's solid and reliable products by cheap sales gimmicks and sensational advertising. He hated him with a consuming passion. The marketing vice-president had no strong feelings about his colleague but regarded him as dull and stubborn. The president, an engineer with a flair for marketing, respected and liked both men and never understood why he found it so difficult to bring them together. When, at long last, he made a determined effort to do so, the marketing vice-president resigned and left the company.

Breaks in communication occur at all organizational levels, but the manager is most likely to be aware of those in which he is directly involved and finds himself either avoiding, or being avoided by, a subordinate.

Although it is often possible to short-circuit a break in communication so that the organizational program goes on without apparent disturbance, every such break promises trouble sooner or later and should be repaired if possible. The conventional method of repairing a break is to bring the parties together in the presence of their common superior for an airing of mutual grievances. Once in a while, when the antagonism or fear that keeps the parties apart derives from a misunderstanding, this method actually works. An alternative is to "knock their heads together," threatening both parties with dire penalties unless they make some effort to resolve their differences. When both methods fail, the manager will find himself confronted with what appears to be a clash of incompatible personalities and he will be tempted to interpret the behavior of one or both parties as neurotic. This interpretation will be especially plausible if his "head-knocking" has put the parties under such psychological strain that they are indeed behaving abnormally. But this is not a helpful guide to further action. Digging a little deeper, the manager will discover that in addition to their supposed incompatibility, the people who refuse to communicate have substantial differences of interest imposed upon them by their positions in the organizational structure, so that at least one of them cannot interact freely with the other without jeopardizing his own interests or those of a faction he represents.

Surprisingly often, the clash of interests is due to some indecision of the manager. In the case described above, the breach between the two vice-presidents reflected the president's inability to choose between a conservative and a flamboyant marketing policy. This indecision encouraged his subordinates to pursue incompatible goals. He flattered himself that he was promoting a kind of Hegelian synthesis of opposing ideas—he once compared his role to that of an orchestra conductor balancing the strings against the woodwinds—but rather than orchestrating the two vice-presidents, he inflamed their mutual distrust by giving them inconsistent versions of marketing policy to follow. The important thing that happened when he brought them together to settle their differences was that he discovered which policy he really preferred and reorganized the company accordingly.

The trick of repairing a break in communication is to start with the assumption that the problem is attributable to a managerial error of some kind, and to search for that error first. Sometimes, as in the case cited, the manager who resolves his own indecision will no longer be able to present himself as an impartial arbiter but will throw his weight behind one of the parties, leaving the other party no choice but to get out. But it happens sometimes that the loser in a decision of this kind welcomes the resolution of ambiguity nearly as much as the winner and finds he can live comfortably with the decision. Whether the adjustment is smooth or not, the organization is usually better off after the break has been repaired.

Once in a long while, the most careful scrutiny of a break in communication between two persons who are supposed to cooperate will not discover any managerial error, but simply some brew of jealousy, irascibility, ethnic prejudice, or private grudge. In such cases, the old formula for conciliation outlined in the *Book of Common Prayer* is a good procedure to follow, making it clear to those concerned that if they insist on pursuing their private feuds they will be excluded from the organization:

The same order shall the Minister use with those, betwixt whom he perceiveth malice and hatred to reign; not suffering them to be partakers of the Lord's Table, until he know them to be reconciled.

And if one of the parties, so at variance, be content to forgive from the bottom of his heart all that the other has trespassed against him, and to make amends for that wherein he himself hath offended, and the other party will not be persuaded to a godly unity, but remain still in his frowardness and malice; the Minister in that case ought to admit the penitent person to the Holy Communion and not him that is obstinate.

An entirely different way of repairing breaks in communication between organizational positions is to shift people around until they sort themselves into compatible pairs. Daniel Katz provides the following illustration:

When Studebaker introduced a new assembly line years ago, there was conflict between union and management over what the new rates should be. The problem was handled by simply rotating all the foremen and stewards on the new line until they got a foreman-steward combination that could agree on the rates that should be set.[15]

Nonverbal communication

Nonverbal messages often contain more information than verbal messages, and nonverbal communication by managers is particularly effective. Since the manager is more closely observed than other members of the organization, the messages implicit in his gestures, displays, and actions are more effectively transmitted. Because he has more freedom of movement within the organization's territory and more autonomy in arranging the personal space around him, he has, in effect, a larger nonverbal vocabulary than other people. His role in organizational rituals of various kinds requires others to imitate him, and in addition he can specify gestures, displays, and actions in which he may not be imitated.

This last sounds more abstruse than it is. In most organizations, the manager's salary cannot be matched or exceeded by any other salary; hence, the manager who sets his own salary imposes an upper limit on all salaries paid by the organization. The size and furnishings of his office, the cost of his company car, the length of his vacation, and the extent of his outside affiliations are all likely to have the similar effect of setting limits to the pretensions of his subordinates. He is always, in some ways, what David Riesman calls a "Captain of Consumption."[16]

It is almost impossible to enumerate all the ways in which nonverbal messages can be conveyed, but the most important media include spatial arrangements, movements from one place to another, appearances and nonappearances at ceremonies, allotments of time, security measures, sociability patterns, personal gestures, clothing, and the entourage taken into various situations. The variety of these media make nonverbal communication highly entertaining for those involved, but there is always some danger of being misunderstood or of showing more than one wants to tell. It would be laborious to look at each medium of nonverbal expression separately, but we can get a pretty good idea of how they work by examining a few types from the standpoint of a manager who understands their possibilities—for example, the microgeography of office buildings, expressive movements in conferences, and the control of behavior by example.

THE MICROGEOGRAPHY OF OFFICE BUILDINGS

Microgeography is the study of the space surrounding individuals and small groups. The microgeography of an office building includes physical structure, floor plans, the location of people and facilities, and the flow of internal traffic.

The physical structure of a building affects any social system housed within it. Tall buildings favor hierarchical relations, but interfere with lateral communications among related departments. Low flat buildings have the opposite effect. A building with a single main entrance encourages a sense of organizational identity, which a building with multiple entrances dispels.

Consider a twelve-story structure that houses the headquarters of a single organization. If the manager's office is placed on the top floor—as it is likely to be, for the advantages of quiet, privacy, and view—the entire building will tend to fall into a hierarchical pattern with the status of individuals and departments measured by their distance from the top. The top floor will take on a hushed, unearthly atmosphere and access to it will be heavily guarded by elevator operators and receptionists. The next two or three floors will imitate the luxury and exclusiveness of the top floor as far as their means allow. Fantastic rumors about "life at the top" will circulate in the lower depths and the occupants of the top floors will be too isolated to supervise lower-floor activities effectively.

If the offices of the manager and his principal assistants are located on the ground floor, location on higher floors will have no automatic significance and the isolation of top management from the organization will be avoided. But some of the departments located on upper floors will become independent mountain kingdoms, jealous of their autonomy and inaccessible to people from other parts of the organization.

In order to get the widest control, the manager's office should be placed in the middle part of the building, but the top floor should be reserved for such facilities as conference rooms, recreation, an executive dining room, or the organization's library. Such a pattern stretches both managerial and rank and file traffic along the whole height of the building and discourages the development of isolated enclaves. It permits the manager to see his subordinates in their own offices as often, or more often, than he invites them to his own. It also enables the manager and his staff to move about the building in their daily routines and to inspect an organizational activity without creating a disturbance.

This sort of thing is elementary, although often neglected in architectural design. A much more complicated microgeographical problem is how to locate all the parts of an organization in a building without unintentionally creating barriers that interfere with essential work, or creating channels of access that encourage illicit activities.

One early microgeographical study described a group of file clerks who, without any particular intention, had been put into an alcove in a very large office. Their file cabinets partly blocked the entrance to the alcove and a fire door gave them private access to a rear corridor. In a relatively short time, the clerks assigned to the alcove became a privileged and cohesive elite who held themselves aloof from the canaille in the outer office, ignoring their supervisor and running their affairs to suit themselves. When, eventually, they were taken out of the alcove and placed elsewhere in the same office, they fortified themselves within a new and larger wall of file cabinets and resisted the reduction of their privileges with astonishing ferocity. The problem was not resolved until nearly all the members of the original group had been replaced.

Generally speaking, a physical barrier between two groups of people in an organization can be counted on to create a corresponding social barrier and to confer a status advantage on whoever controls passage through the barrier. Where there is no barrier at all to mark a division between groups, as when the secretaries of unrelated departments are placed in the same stenographic pool, there is likely to be a much freer flow of information than the organization intends. If the building is redesigned to eliminate all corner offices but one, making storerooms out of the other three corners, proximity to the remaining corner office may become so important a mark of status that every new arrival or departure causes an agonizing round of musical chairs. If all the offices on a floor are of identical size, the occupants of corner offices will be privileged, but isolated from each other. The matching of rooms, corridors, distances, and lines of sight to an intended pattern of organizational relationships is an unending jigsaw puzzle. In a large organization it can never be completely solved, but approximate solutions can be found by both careful planning and trial and error.

EXPRESSIVE MOVEMENTS IN CONFERENCES

The study of expressive movements—body placement, gestures, and other body signs—is another trivial branch of social science that every responsible manager ought to study. Since the manager of an organization is excluded from full participation in the grapevine and has only limited information about the private sentiments of subordinates, he must often rely on his unaided observation to discover what everybody else in the organization already knows. On the other hand, he has exceptional opportunities for observation because he sees so many people and can often choose the setting in which he sees them.

Consider the opportunities for observation in the routine conference a manager might hold with six or seven subordinates. The order of arrival is significant. Early arrival generally signifies eagerness to participate, and lateness or absence usually indicates some reluctance connected with the business at hand, or some

Table 10: Tactical features of a conference table

MANAGER

BEST LOCATION FOR
GIVING A ROUTINE REPORT

BEST LOCATION FOR
A NEWCOMER

BEST LOCATION FOR
PRESENTING A NEW IDEA

BEST LOCATION FOR A
STRONG SUBORDINATE

BEST LOCATION FOR
STARTING A FIGHT

BEST LOCATION FOR
A WEAK SUBORDINATE

BEST LOCATION FOR AN
OUTSIDE OBSERVER

DOOR

mistrust of the other participants. People who arrive together and deep in conversation are either announcing a coalition or concealing a quarrel.

The selection of seats is significant. Even in a meeting with fixed seating arrangements, small variations—a place skipped, a chair shoved to one side or the other—are significant. People who crowd close to the chairman are likely to be seeking his support. Those who isolate themselves at the other end of the table may be girding for battle. A real fight, as distinct from a difference of opinion, usually aligns people into visible factions. Positions at the end of a long table or in the middle of a side are taken by people who intend to participate actively, while the corners are occupied by those who want to remain inconspicuous.

For a period of some years I attended business conferences in a room with an oval table and an equal number of black chairs and white chairs. There was a feeble standing joke about the good guys sitting in white chairs and the bad guys in black chairs, but, joke or not, several odd little patterns developed out of the necessity for each participant to choose a black or a white chair at the beginning of each meeting. The white chairs came to be associated with optimism, growth, and good news, and the black chairs with disapproval, reorganization, and financial stringency. Participants in this way signaled in advance the general tone of their contribution to a particular meeting. People on the same side of a controversial issue were likely to select like-colored chairs. The occasional efforts of an individual to adopt one color or the other permanently and thus avoid the choice were detected by the other participants and subjected to the kind of pointed joking by which violations of etiquette are corrected.

Such expressive movements as gestures, smiles and frowns, placement of arms and legs, seated posture, fiddling and doodling, scratching and yawning, crossed glances, the direction of attention toward or away from a speaker, tones of voice, and the length and character of silences, serve in any meeting to amplify and clarify what is said and may indeed be more informative than any of the words spoken. The first thing for a manager to do in a conference is to look and to listen; if these demanding activities keep him from talking as much as he would like, so much the better.

BEHAVIOR CONTROL BY EXAMPLE

The norms of any organization consist largely of informal expectations and unstated rules. The manager, as keeper of the collective conscience, often has more power to modify informal norms and to enact new ones than he could ever acquire with respect to the organization's written rules and regulations. This power is perhaps most readily exercised with respect to the norms that say what a member owes to the organization and what he may legitimately take from it.

In an enterprise with regular working hours, say 9:00 to 5:00 with lunch from 12:00 to 1:00, the manager's working schedule is likely to determine what hours are kept by all the people who do not punch time clocks and by some of those who do. If it is his habit to come in about 10:30, be out to lunch from 12:00 to 2:00, and leave the office around 4:00, most of his higher-ranking subordinates will probably come to work after 9:00 and leave before 5:00, spacing their comings and goings so that a subordinate is generally present when his superior arrives and when he leaves. Lunch hours will be less regularly distributed but will certainly average more than an hour. These departures from the working schedule will sacrifice hundreds or thousands of working hours without any compensating benefit. They will have some deleterious effect on the self-esteem of the executives who cheat a little on their hours, and on the morale of the rank-and-file workers who are compelled to arrive and leave on time. No amount of exhortation will make much difference, but the manager can change the situation overnight by coming in at 9:00, lunching from 12:00 to 1:00, and leaving at 5:00. Within a week, most of the organization will be on that schedule and will remain on it as long as he does.

If the manager chooses to come in at 8:00 and to leave at 6:00, the effect will be less salutary. By following the official schedule, he creates an expectation that everybody else will do so. When he exceeds it, he does not create any clear expectation for others (except perhaps for his personal assistants) but merely identifies himself as a fanatical worker. This will certainly have some influence on the time schedule of other members of the organization, but all that can be reliably predicted is that they will put in longer hours than if he came in late and left early.

A manager can usually enforce any sumptuary rule he is willing to follow himself. The manager who logs his personal telephone calls and reimburses the organization for them will find it fairly easy to prevent other people from charging personal calls to the organization; otherwise, the practice may be irrepressible.

If the manager travels economy class, no one in the organization is likely to buy first-class tickets; it will not even be necessary to formulate a rule. If he has a small, inexpensive official car, no one else in the organization will feel entitled to a limousine; if he has a limousine with a chauffeur, he will sooner or later have to concede either part-time limousines or unchauffeured luxury cars to his principal subordinates.

The corporation or union or government executive who dazzles his subordinates by his jet planes and fast boats, his rosewood desk and his office tapestries, his official trips to Samarkand and the Riviera, and the costliness of his Christmas cards, may think he reads admiration in their eyes; what he really sees is a glint of matching greed.

How to recognize effective communication

The volume of communication and the degree of consensus required to hold an organization together differ from one setting to another, but the manager who has achieved effective communication will generally observe that:

1. The routine operational reports that reach him are seldom late and never falsified.

2. When he asks for a special report on some phase of the organizational program, he is never told that the information exists but cannot be assembled without excessive trouble or expense.

3. His own formulations of organizational policies and problems are often repeated back to him by other people.

4. He seldom finds himself in disagreement with the priorities assigned to problems by his subordinates.

5. He is usually comfortable at meetings and conferences within the organization, whether he presides himself or attends as a visitor.

6. When he engages in consultation about a problem, he invariably learns new and important things, but they are not the kind of new things that make him change his whole picture of the organization.

7. When he makes an important decision, the grapevine is likely to carry the news throughout the organization before an official announcement can be made.

8. The public speeches and actions of representatives of the organization seldom embarrass him.

9. His subordinates often suggest a plan he has been turning over in his mind, or install a new procedure he has been about to suggest.

10. There are many things going on in the organization that he knows nothing about, but they do not make him apprehensive.

11. The relatively few grievances that come to him can be promptly and vigorously handled without disrupting the organization.

12. He has very few secrets, and those he has can be safely confided to his close associates.

13. He has no regular talebearers or stool pigeons within the organization, and does not want any.

14. There is no part of the organization from which he cannot obtain routine communications or which fails to respond to routine communications from him.

15. Misunderstandings and mistakes in communication between himself and various parts of the organization occur quite frequently, but do not go undetected for long.

3:Productivity

The bottleneck is at the top of the bottle.
AN OLD SAYING

Efficiency and effectiveness

Every organization has work to do in the real world and some way of measuring how well that work is done. The responsibility of a manager is to see that the work gets done as efficiently and effectively as possible, whether it consists of producing goods, winning games, teaching pupils, preventing crimes, defending a frontier, making scientific discoveries, staging an entertainment, or any of the myriad other tasks that organizations undertake. The devices that measure efficiency and effectiveness are as diverse as the tasks themselves, but are inescapable from the manager's standpoint; he must ordinarily accept the conventional yardsticks, whatever they are. If the organization is a retail store, he cannot decide to disregard profitability; if it is a professional baseball team, he cannot replace the number of games won and lost with some other measure of performance more to his liking. He can, and often will, introduce additional measures of performance to move the organizational program in one direction or another, but these are not likely to have much effect unless the conventional yardsticks are satisfied at the same time.

The conventional yardsticks of performance cover both efficiency and effectiveness. An organization is *efficient* if, compared to similar organizations, its output is relatively high in relation to its input. It is *effective* if it achieves its intended goals. An organization may be highly effective without being especially efficient. Some victorious armies have been very wasteful. An organization may also be very efficient without being effective. Some declining businesses are models of operating efficiency. Efficiency and effectiveness are closely related but they are not interchangeable.

Although efficiency and effectiveness are both important, effectiveness is more important. In the numerous situations that require a choice between them, it is generally advisable to make some sacrifice of efficiency for the sake of higher effectiveness, provided that the organization's survival is not thereby jeopardized. Most good managers grasp this principle intuitively, but it is helpful, even for them, to understand the reasons for it.

THE ORGANIZATION AS A QUASI-MACHINE

Every human organization can be described as if it were a machine. It is designed for a particular purpose and composed of specialized moving parts. It absorbs energy and materials and converts them into other forms. It requires both routine maintenance and emergency repairs. From time to time some critical part breaks down and the organization ceases to function until the broken part is repaired or replaced.

In some other ways, an organization is spectacularly unlike a real machine. Its specialized moving parts—people—are incapable of behaving in a fully mechanical way even on an assembly line or in a marching band—incapable and unwilling. The human parts of an organization never do exactly what the organization wants them to do. Each of them has purposes of his own that are incongruent with those of the organization, and each of them participates in the organizational program in an intermittent and individual way.

The various subgroups that make up an organization are similarly unreliable. They, too, have goals that are inconsistent with those of the whole organization. Nearly every department and section, for example, seeks to enhance its own relative importance, even when that involves a loss of efficiency or effectiveness for the organization.

To put it as plainly as possible, the human organization, as a quasi-machine, seldom runs as smoothly as a real machine in good working order. At any given time, some of the quasi-machine's parts are practicing what Thorstein Veblen called "the conscientious withdrawal of efficiency," and other parts are engaged in sabotage, an old French word that originally meant trampling on the product of one's labor with wooden shoes.

On the other hand, no real machine is as effective as a quasi-machine for the accomplishment of tasks under changing conditions. Being human, the quasi-machine can restructure itself as it goes along. The individual parts of which it is composed develop new functions on their own initiative. The interaction between them may lead to coordinated efforts of great subtlety and power.

The operator of a quasi-machine has two recurrent problems: how to keep the thing from falling apart and how to get more work out of it than it is supposedly capable of. What he does to solve these problems is called supervision in some organizations and leadership in others, the latter term being generally preferred in organizations, such as armies and orchestras, that cannot be certain of achieving their goals. Because of that uncertainty and the excitement it produces, a great deal of attention is concentrated on the individual at the top, and regardless of his personal characteristics he assumes, if successful, the charisma that seems to separate leadership from mere supervision. "I have observed," writes David Ogilvy, "that no creative organization, whether it is a research laboratory, a magazine, a Paris kitchen, or an advertising agency, will produce a great body of work unless it is led by a *formidable* individual."[1] But formidable or not, a charismatic leader, like any other responsible manager, gets the work out by supervising people.

Modes of supervision

There are two general modes of supervision: direct and indirect. They are governed by different principles. Many managerial positions involve a continuous shuttling between these modes. In theory, direct supervision presents fewer problems than indirect supervision since it is less dependent upon third parties. In practice, direct supervision requires more concentration and longer practice, and it is more often botched.

PRINCIPLES OF DIRECT SUPERVISION

1. *Set unmistakable goals.* The first step in getting any kind of work done under direct supervision is to make clear what the work is for, why it needs to be done in a particular way, and what constitutes success in its performance. Even in the most elementary collective tasks, it is unreasonable to assume that either the purposes of the task or the desired standards of performance are too obvious to require explanation. In almost every successful performance of a group task, goals and standards must be set in advance, clearly communicated, kept constantly in view, and dramatized along the way.

Goal-setting is easiest in elite organizations—the great research laboratory, the three-star restaurant kitchen, the world-renowned orchestra, the champion athletic team—where maximum excellence is sought and everyone expects the supervisor to demand infinite pains for the sake of excellence. Goal-setting is more difficult in mediocre organizations, and it is often useful to concentrate on one aspect of the work for the sake of overall improvement. I knew a man who ran the typing pool in a large engineering firm and supervised a dozen typists who turned out endless pages of reports and specifications. One day, at the sight of several typists using their erasers at the same time, he was moved to announce that from then on he would demand perfect, error-free typing. Corrections and erasures would no longer be permitted. Erasers were to be thrown away. The typist who made a mistake of any kind was to discard that page and start again. The first few days of the new system were marked by tears, protests, and a great waste of paper. Thereafter, the error rate declined to a negligible level and stayed there as long as that supervisor remained in charge and was able to explain to each new recruit that the goal was perfect, error-free typing.

2. *Supervise the work more than the worker.* The essence of

supervised work is that whatever the worker produces comes to the attention of the supervisor, so that every improvement or deterioration in the quality of work (or in the quality of supervision) is noticed and stimulates appropriate feedback. The chef who sits at the kitchen door and tastes every dish as it passes, the office manager who scans every typed page before it goes out, the farmer who looks at the new bales of hay and counts them and checks over the mowing machine and the baler at the end of the day, all find it easy to communicate with their workers.

Supervising the worker is another matter entirely. The unnecessary exercise of personal authority is a kind of sabotage ceaselessly practiced by incompetent supervisors. Most people need a zone of freedom around them in order to work well. It is hard to find anyone, no matter how meek or discouraged, who willingly submits to a tighter control than the necessities of the work require.

3. *Distinguish between essential and nonessential rules.* There is an old textbook distinction in sociology between *folkways*, which are convenient and recognized social practices, and *mores*, which are the rules that hold a society together. Every work group has its own folkways and mores, and the supervisor is responsible for keeping them distinct. If he is clear in his own mind about which rules are essential and which are not, he is not likely to fritter away his authority in efforts to get perfect compliance with rules such as "No Smoking" or "All tools must be returned to the tool crib by the end of the day."*

But with respect to those few norms that express the organization's moral commitments and do call for perfect compliance, the supervisor's best course is to treat every violation as harshly as his powers allow. Ogilvy provides this edifying example from his experience in the kitchen of a great French restaurant:

> Soon after I joined M. Pitard's brigade, I was faced with a problem of morality for which neither my father nor my schoolmasters had prepared me. The *chef garde-manger* sent me to the *chef saucier* with some raw sweetbreads which smelled so putrid that

---

* If for some special reason it *is* essential to repress smoking or get all tools returned to the tool crib, the problem must be approached less authoritatively—for example, by calling all those concerned into a conference to discuss their reasons for noncompliance.

I knew they would endanger the life of any client who ate them; the sauce would mask their condition, and the client would eat them. I protested to the *chef garde-manger*, but he told me to carry out his order; he knew that he would be in hot water if M. Pitard discovered that he had run out of fresh sweetbreads. What was I to do? I had been brought up to believe that it was dishonorable to inform. But I did just that. I took the putrid sweetbreads to M. Pitard and invited him to smell them. He did so and, without a word to me, went over to the *chef garde-manger* and fired him on the spot. This poor bastard had to leave, then and there.[2]

4. *Reward sparingly; punish much more sparingly.* The usual form of reward in work groups is praise. The usual form of punishment is criticism. Public praise or public criticism have much higher intensity, of course, than praise or criticism in private. Other forms of reward and punishment are raises and pay reductions, bonuses and fines, promotions and demotions, the extension and withdrawal of privileges.

It can usually be observed in an organized group that the aversion to a given punishment is greater than the desire for an equivalent reward. This can be demonstrated with laboratory precision by anyone who controls a payroll. Step 1: raise everybody's wages by 10 percent. The effect on productivity and morale will be nearly imperceptible. Step 2: after an interval of weeks or months, lower the same wages by 5 percent. The effect on productivity and morale will be disastrous.

All sorts of variations on this unwise experiment can be devised. For example, raising the wages of part of a work group can be counted on to demoralize those who are not raised. But the point need not be labored. A reduction of pay or privileges or status amounts to a reduction in the ability of the worker to obtain satisfaction through the organization and, inasmuch as he prefers satisfaction to frustration, he is bound to resist. Individuals in organized groups seldom evaluate their rewards and punishments in absolute terms; they are much more likely to measure what they receive by comparison with what others receive. Hence, to bestow a reward on one worker is often to impose a punishment on his peers. Even casual praise may have this unintended effect.

The unintended effects of punishments are even more severe

than those of rewards. A punishment, if effective, undermines the
position of the victim in his work group and thereby reduces his
capacity for effective cooperation. It may also reduce the status of
his friends and peers, with remote and harmful repercussions.

The foregoing observations are not meant to suggest that rewards and punishments should be withheld, but only that they
must always be administered with great caution. For example,
praise and criticism ought generally to be private rather than public, and understated rather than overstated. Major rewards ought
to be reserved for those whose right to them is universally recognized. Major punishments, as a general rule, should not be imposed on persons who are still potentially useful to the organization.

The foregoing warnings do not apply to rewards and punishments that are thoroughly routinized. By all means compliment the
pastry chef on his chocolate éclairs *if* the quality of his work is such
that you will surely be able to praise his deep-dish apple pie tomor-
row and his brioches the day after.

5. *Give credit where credit is due*. This principle looks simple,
but to apply it correctly you need a rather complicated formula for
allotting credit and blame, which goes as follows:

Success should be credited to the entire group, or divided
between the entire group and one or more of its members. Failure
should be blamed on the supervisor alone or on the supervisor and
the entire group jointly.

The rationale for this formula is that the supervisor, having set
out to elicit a collective effort from a group, must necessarily credit
the group as a whole if that effort is successful. He may in addition
acknowledge the special contributions of individuals, but he cannot take any credit himself for the collective effort, being the
outsider who called it forth.

If the collective effort is not forthcoming, the manager must
accept responsibility for having been unable to call it forth, since
that was his primary task. He may or may not implicate the group
as a whole in the failure, but he cannot blame individual members
of the group without assigning them a responsibility for the collective effort equal to his own, which would amount to his abdication.

6. *Listen to complaints sympathetically; never complain in*

turn. A little reflection will show you that this follows automatically from the previous principle.

7. *Defend the faith.* The manager of an organization, as we have seen, is the natural custodian of its sacred symbols and the keeper of its moral character. Translated to the level of a group, this means that the supervisor must take the group and its work more seriously than anyone else and know how to assume a ceremonial stance for great occasions. He may be cynical and worldly-wise about anything else he pleases, provided he shows an innocent and trusting faith in the value of the collective activity that he supervises. If he lacks that faith, and cannot simulate it, he might as well give up and go into some other line of work.

8. *Develop an inner circle.* From the supervisor's standpoint, an inner circle of lieutenants provides additional eyes, ears, and hands to do his supervising. From the rank and file standpoint, the interposition of an intermediary who is partly a supervisor and partly a colleague makes it easier and safer to express complaints, suggestions, and requests. Traditional work groups almost always have an inner circle. But a circle ought to have at least three members. *"Tres faciunt collegium,"* said a maxim of Roman law; it takes three to make an inner circle. If the group is too small to support an inner circle of three, the supervisor had better consider doing the job alone. A single lieutenant, or even two, may be more hindrance than help.

9. *Protect the status of subordinates.* Even a small work group without a formal hierarchy does not consist of an undifferentiated rank and file. There are usually significant differences in title, seniority, technical qualifications, and authority within any group. Although it is not always immediately apparent, all of these statuses are part of the same structure from which the supervisor derives his own authority, so that unless he respects the prerogatives of his subordinates and insists that others respect them also, he undermines himself.

10. *Retain final control.* If, as a supervisor, you develop an inner circle of lieutenants and protect their prerogatives as well as those of other subordinates, you may discover one day that you are unable to decide anything on your own. To avoid that, you need to retain an unshared right to approve (or veto) expenditures and

personnel actions. You do not need to initiate them; you *do* need more than token control of them. Unless you have enough power to make independent decisions about financial and personnel matters, you do not have enough power for effective supervision. It may even be necessary to act capriciously now and then in order to demonstrate your ability to do so.

11. *Innovate democratically.* Even the most traditional organizations require a surprisingly high rate of innovation to stay in touch with technological and environmental changes. In many cases, the introduction of innovations is the principal part of a supervisor's job. It is always a hazardous part. There are more ways of coming to grief while innovating than can be readily counted, and some of the practices that otherwise contribute to effective supervision must be suspended here.

The effects of an innovation are always somewhat unpredictable. In default of omniscience, the supervisor needs to obtain as much information as possible from all the people who will be affected by the innovation and who have facts or insights about its possible consequences. Because any innovation in an organization affects some people adversely, or seems to, some resistance must always be anticipated and the possibility of sabotage is never remote. Thus, every innovation, however trivial, needs as much support as can conveniently be mustered. As both field and laboratory experiments have shown, the way to muster support for an innovation is to bring all the people affected by it into its planning at an early stage and to give them a voice in the various decisions that need to be made, from the first to the last stages. Successful innovations are discussed, designed, and implemented in an atmosphere of participatory democracy. This takes a little doing in an otherwise authoritarian organization, but it is always worth the trouble.

12. *Take infinite pains.* This is the most important principle of direct supervision, and the most difficult to learn. Some people seem to come by it naturally; others acquire the habit by experience and practice. Inborn or learned, it is what distinguishes genius from mere competence and the great team from a mediocre one. The inimitable M. Pitard stationed himself at the waiters' counter and inspected each dish before it left the kitchen. Some dishes he sent back to the kitchen for more work.

Anyone who has ever heard a major symphony orchestra rehearsing for a concert will have noticed that much of the rehearsal time was spent on nuances of interpretation by subordinate instruments that could not possibly be noticed by the concert audience. Similarly, Paul Strand, doing a documentary film about a Malay fishing village, postponed the shooting of the final scene for a month because one fisherman got a haircut, and Strand was unwilling to go on with the scene until the fisherman's hair was the same length as it had been in a previous scene.

THE CONTRAST BETWEEN DIRECT AND INDIRECT SUPERVISION

Indirect supervision always involves the direct supervision of immediate subordinates, and, as we shall presently see, some of the same principles apply to both modes of supervision. The differences, however, are as important as the similarities. It happens very often that people who have been promoted to high positions because of a talent for direct supervision fail miserably at indirect supervision. The reverse case is less common but not excessively rare. Some highly successful managers of great organizations have been notably inept at direct supervision—for example, the first Henry Ford.

The most important feature of indirect supervision is limited power. The indirect supervisor does not have the means to shape the organization to his heart's desire, or even to understand it thoroughly. The basic patterns of work activity, the division of labor, the customs of the milieu, are constraints he cannot disregard and cannot easily change.

The medium and large organizations whose managers engage in indirect supervision are extremely diverse in structure and in patterns of authority. Moreover, the managers of organizations that look superficially alike differ greatly in power, depending upon their personal traits, the support they can muster in various constituencies, and the prerogatives of a particular position. But even the best situated indirect supervisor—the head of a family-owned corporation or a chief of state supported by a majority party—has an imperfect and uneven control of the organization for which he is responsible. Many of its functions remain entirely beyond his reach, because they admit no interference or are not amenable to inspection or have independent bases of power. The president of a university, for example, cannot effectively supervise the conduct of teaching and research in any academic department. He can only exercise some marginal long-term control over individual departments by means of budgetary policy. In other large-scale organizations, such as manufacturing companies, fewer enclaves are protected by professional privilege, but departments have various efficacious ways of repelling what they regard as managerial interference. When such challenges to authority become too obtrusive to overlook, they provoke a reorganization.

Reorganization often takes the form of decentralization, following a formula first devised by Alfred Sloan for General Motors in the early 1920s and later imitated by innumerable other corporations and noncommercial institutions. The story of Sloan's reorganization of General Motors is told by Alfred Chandler in his "Strategy and Structure."[3] After more than half a century, the Sloan formula still has an air of freshness and novelty and still represents an "advanced" as compared to a "conservative" management philosophy. The reason may be that the formula is genuinely paradoxical, giving much greater autonomy to subordinate managers with one hand while gripping them much more tightly with the other.

The general managers of the operating divisions of General Motors were in effect set up in business for themselves.

> The General Manager formulates all the policies for his particular unit, subject only to the executive control of the President. The responsibility of the head of each unit is absolute and he is looked upon to exercise his full initiative and ability in developing his particular operation to the fullest possible extent and to assume the full responsibility of success or failure.[4]

But this grant of independence had two new and important strings attached. Uniform accounting procedures were established for the entire company, and each operating unit was required to follow them without deviation, so that its financial situation was completely and continuously visible to the central office. (Some other companies, and at a later time General Motors, also imposed uniform personnel procedures and reserved certain spheres of activity, such as litigation and foreign marketing, for the central office.)

Within the framework of uniform accounts, each operating unit was required to submit annual, seasonal, and monthly forecasts of purchases, production, inventory, and sales to the central office, where they were reviewed and occasionally revised. As the authority for routine operations was decentralized, the central office was vastly enlarged by the appointment of group vice-presidents and other executives exclusively engaged in "policy-making," and by the development of an elaborate structure of special-purpose committees to coordinate planning and operations.

The independence conferred upon operating divisions under this plan was not entirely illusory. In many respects they functioned as separate businesses, competing with each other, buying from and selling to each other at something like market prices, and developing their own network of commercial contacts with suppliers and dealers. But at the same time, the new financial controls enabled the central office to monitor operations very closely, and the enlarged size and weight of the central office enabled it to step in and reorganize an operating unit, or on occasion to abolish or merge operating units, without encountering much resistance. A similar formula—increased autonomy and self-determination on the one hand, uniform accounting and tight monitoring of performance on the other—was eventually extended to the shop floor in most large American corporations by means of such devices as shop conferences, sensitivity training, and job enlargement programs.

The exercise of indirect supervision is obviously different in a decentralized organization from that in a pyramidal organization of the military type or in a federal organization whose component units are more or less equal. The principles of indirect supervision, consequently, are more variable than the principles of direct supervision outlined a few pages back. Effective indirect supervision is much more dependent on time, place, and circumstances. What works well in one situation may be disastrous in another, as admirals discover when they try to run colleges and as industrial executives learn in government agencies. Nevertheless, there are certain general principles that do appear to apply to all types of indirect supervision.

PRINCIPLES OF INDIRECT SUPERVISION

1. *Find and hold the purse strings.* Without fiscal control, an indirect supervisor is helpless.

2. *Develop detailed plans and projections.* The object is to measure the performance of every operating unit in a given time period against a prior projection, making sure that the comparison is clearly visible to all concerned.

3. *Develop personal relationships with subordinate managers.* This may be done either inside or outside the organizational setting. It is desirable for sheer human comfort and essential in order to obtain adequate information about matters not covered by measures of performance or output.

4. *Do your homework.* The indirect supervisor is necessarily deficient, compared to a direct supervisor, in firsthand knowledge of the operations for which he is responsible. This natural handicap should be compensated by a mastery of the wider information he can obtain by virtue of his position.

5. *Roam the streets.* Haroun Al-Raschid, you remember, was the caliph of Baghdad who roamed the streets of his capital in disguise to find out how well his government was functioning. Disguise may or may not be practicable, but an indirect supervisor needs always to overcome his shyness and to look at the lower depths of his domain with his own eyes.

6. *Reorganize drastically or not at all.* It is nearly impossible for an indirect supervisor to transform an existing social structure from his position above and outside it. Operating units whose performance or output is unsatisfactory and cannot be improved by routine measures should be disbanded and replaced. The indirect supervisor usually finds it easier to carry through a drastic reorganization than to fiddle with minor reforms against the entrenched resistance of an uncooperative unit.

7. *Respect successful operations.* This is the corollary of the preceding principle. A unit that is exceptionally productive and does not interfere with other units should be left alone if possible, even when some aspects of its operation appear unnecessary or crazy. When someone complained to Abraham Lincoln that General Grant had been drunk throughout a successful engagement,

the President asked to know what brand of whiskey Grant favored so that he might send some to his other generals.

8. *Refrain from attempting the impossible.* No indirect supervisor is omnipotent; most are pitifully weak in relation to their organizational ambitions, and the larger and more powerful the organization, the less likely that it will respond obediently to its master's voice. The most important principle of indirect supervision is to concentrate effort on goals that lie within reach and to waste as little effort as possible on the worthier goals that are unattainable.

This last rule, baldly stated, seems ignoble and invites further explanation. The mythology of organizations includes a good deal of hyperbole and boasting. Unrealistic aspirations are often praised as if they were equivalent to real accomplishments. This sort of rhetoric is useful in hopeless situations—for example, in the campaign of a political candidate who has no chance of winning an election. It helps the participants in such an exercise to carry out their responsibilities gracefully—and of course, miracles do occur. Indeed, the manager of a large organization is never well advised to be openly cynical about his prospects. But since he has more to gain from organizational success than anyone else, and more to lose from organizational failure, it is generally better for him to promote collective aspirations that lie within the limits of the possible than to encourage hopes that are certain to be disappointed.

9. *Innovate boldly, but not often.* It follows from the foregoing discussion that the indirect supervisor has only a limited ability to jar an organization out of its groove of custom. To do so at all, he must make some changes, but all changes are, from his standpoint, costly and time-consuming. They arouse resistance and have unintended effects, which he is seldom in a position to anticipate completely or even to understand fully after they have occurred. On the other hand, since all innovations are potentially dangerous, there is no reason to make piddling ones.

The risk of innovating can be considerably mitigated by extensive consultation and by the development of as much consensus as possible throughout the organization before, during, and after the introduction of a new rule, a new piece of equipment, a new procedure, or a new policy. Consultation works much better when it is genuine; that is, when the advice of the consultees is heeded and the proposed innovation is modified accordingly. But even insincere consultation is much better than none at all. People whose advice has been sought are much more likely to accept an innovation than those who have no advance knowledge of it at all. Moreover, the development of channels for consultation within an organization seems to make the next innovation much easier, and may even, under very favorable conditions, lead to a happy pattern of engineering from below.

Let us turn now to consider some of the problems that every indirect supervisor encounters as he attempts to use his limited authority to maximize productivity.

Maximizing productivity

The organization, as we keep saying, is not really a machine, because it is composed of living people, but it functions in some respects like a machine, because it is a set of interlocking parts designed for a particular purpose. Regarding it as a quasi-machine, the operator is led to ask a number of questions about its potential productivity, for example: What is the organization's potential output under existing conditions? or, How much could potential output be raised by the installation of new equipment or the installation of new procedures?

These same questions come up in connection with real machines and are moderately difficult to answer. They are much more difficult to answer for a quasi-machine, primarily because the human parts resist being operated at maximum capacity. This resistance is both obvious and subtle, both individual and social, both deliberate and unconscious. Overcoming it is the principal activity of the indirect supervisor, and he must use both open and devious methods.

ESTIMATING POTENTIAL PRODUCTIVITY

There are two rough but useful methods for arriving at a preliminary estimate of the maximum capacity of an organization. The estimates obtained by these methods are almost invariably low because they cannot allow for unknown improvement in existing procedures. But they do provide a starting point.

The first method is to break the work into its elementary components, time them, allow for necessary transitions and interruptions, and then add up those time allowances to determine the normal output in a standard interval of time. If, for example, it is known that a public-opinion interview takes between thirty minutes and an hour, that the average travel time between interviews is approximately thirty minutes, that one hour a day is required to make interview appointments by telephone, and that the average waiting time is fifteen minutes per interview, then the maximum capacity of an interview team can reasonably be estimated at four completed interviews per interviewer per day. If it then appears that a given team averages only two interviews per interviewer per day, then a gap has been established between the team's actual and maximum capacity.

The second method is to compare the average productivity of a working group with its own best performance or with the best performance of a similar group under comparable conditions. Either calculation may give startling results.

I was once asked to estimate the efficiency of a port battalion unloading ships by lighter in a foreign harbor under wartime conditions. This port battalion had received a presidential unit citation for outstanding performance. Comparing the average daily output of each lighter crew in terms of tons of cargo moved with its own best daily performance under standard conditions, we arrived at the startling but verifiable conclusion that the battalion's average productivity ran about 12 percent of its maximum capacity. Further investigation disclosed every conceivable type of work avoidance. Nonetheless, the unit had looked excellent compared to other port battalions whose habits were even more outrageous.

It is not uncommon for a multinational corporation to install an exact duplicate of an existing factory in another country, the difficulties of adaptation being compensated for by savings in plant design and engineering. When such plants are staffed by local workmen and put into operation, it is invariably noted that some departments have very different output rates from their identically equipped prototypes in the original plant. In one instance, the metalworking department of a pump factory in the Netherlands unexpectedly turned out five times as much work as the prototype department back in Ohio.

IMPROVING ACTUAL PRODUCTIVITY

Nearly every productive organization shows conspicuous gaps between actual and potential output in some of its departments. Even after productivity has been systematically studied and improved, some large gaps will persist and new ones will appear. The improvement of productivity is not something that can be done once and for all; it requires constant vigilance.

The reasons that an organization, left to itself, tends to fall further and further below its potential productivity may be conveniently summed up under four headings: defective work methods, output limitations, systematic cheating, and snags in the work flow.

Defective work methods   The causes of defective work methods in apparently efficient industrial organizations were analyzed in the early 1900s by Frederick W. Taylor, the "father of scientific management." Here is one of his classic cases:

The Bethlehem Steel Company had five blast furnaces, the product of which had been handled by a pig-iron gang for many years. This gang, at this time, consisted of about seventy-five men. They were good, average pig-iron handlers, were under an excellent foreman who himself had been a pig-iron handler, and the work was done, on the whole, about as fast and as cheaply as it was anywhere else at that time. . . .

An inclined plank was placed against the side of a car, and each man picked up from his pile a pig of iron weighing about 92 pounds, walked up the inclined plank and dropped it on the end of the car.

We found that this gang were loading on the average about 12½ long tons per man per day. We were surprised to find, after studying the matter, that a first-class pig-iron handler ought to handle between 47 and 48 long tons per day, instead of 12½ tons. This task seemed to us so very large that we were obliged to go over our work several times before we were absolutely sure that we were right. Once we were sure, however, that 47 tons was a proper day's work for a first-class pig-iron handler, the task which

faced us as managers under the modern scientific plan was clearly
before us. It was our duty to see that the 80,000 tons of pig-iron
was loaded on to the cars at the rate of 47 tons per man per day,
in place of 12½ tons, at which rate the work was then being done.
And it was further our duty to see that this work was done without bringing on a strike among the men, without any quarrel with
the men, and to see that the men were happier and better con-
tented when loading at the new rate of 47 tons than they were
when loading at the old rate of 12½ tons.[5]

Taylor's method was to observe the seventy-five men for several days, then pick out and investigate four of the strongest, finally selecting the one who seemed most interested in getting
higher pay. This laborer, Schmidt, was then persuaded to work
under very close supervision in return for a 60 percent increase in
his daily wages. One of Taylor's men stood over him with a stop-
watch all day long saying, "Now pick up the pig and walk, now sit
down and rest, now walk, now rest," until Schmidt got the hang of
it and began to average 47½ tons a day. One worker after another
was picked out and trained to handle pig iron in the same way.
The secret, as Taylor explained it, was that a man doing work this
heavy had to be entirely free from load for more than half of his
working time in order to avoid cumulative muscular fatigue. Previously, Schmidt and his fellows had worked themselves into a
state of exhaustion early in the day by not alternating effort and
rest in a systematic way.

There seem to have been two other reasons for the improvement. First, by demonstrating the feasibility of a much higher
work rate, Taylor changed the idea of all concerned about what
constituted a fair day's work. Second, in the course of his man-by-
man training program, he apparently eliminated those members of
the original crew who were unwilling or unable to keep up with
the new pace.

Stated more generally, Taylor's conclusions were that: (1)
human capabilities in a particular kind of work must be determined experimentally—they are not intuitively obvious, either to
participants or to observers; (2) a worker cannot achieve his maximum capacity at a given job without systematic training, based
upon a prior study of the component steps of the job and the
sequence in which they are performed; (3) to achieve high aver-

age productivity, workers must be carefully selected according to their fitness for a particular kind of work.

The industrial managers of Taylor's time reacted with enthusiasm to these suggestions. Time-and-motion studies, human engineering, and personnel testing flourished. By and large, these new methods were effective in raising productivity, although not quite as effective as their promoters anticipated. Even as Taylor wrote, the nature of industrial work and the composition of the American labor force were changing rapidly. Jobs as simple as Schmidt's were being taken over by conveyor belts and lift trucks. The winding down of immigration and the great increase in secondary education began to narrow the cultural gap between managers and workers. Within a very few years, Taylor's condescension toward Schmidt and his other subjects would sound hopelessly old-fashioned. "The workman who is best suited for handling pig iron," Taylor wrote, "is unable to understand the real science of doing this class of work. He is so stupid that the word 'percentage' has no meaning for him, and he must consequently be trained by a man more intelligent than himself."[6]

Some of Taylor's findings, however, are still valid today. It is still the case that in the absence of continuous job analysis and systematic job training, the output of most workers and work groups does not come anywhere near their maximum capacity, even when they make a maximum effort. But as more was learned about industrial sociology, it became apparent that a number of other factors Taylor had not taken into account also influenced productivity.

Output limitation   The 1920s saw the rise of a new school of industrial experts who advocated the improvement of human relations in the factory as a basic method of improving productivity. Their principal spokesman was Elton Mayo, whose studies at the Hawthorne plant of the Western Electric Company from 1927 to 1932 led to a new managerial ideology, based on the belief that the productivity in any work situation is largely determined by patterns of social interaction among the workers.[7]

The experiments at Western Electric led Mayo and his collaborators to the following conclusions, among others:

1. The economic incentive is not the only motivating force to

which workers respond, and not necessarily the most important.

2. Worker responses to managerial initiative are more often collective than individual.

3. The productivity of an individual worker is always affected by his emotions, which in turn are influenced by the emotions of his peers.

4. Peer groups form in work situations whenever the opportunity offers. They control production by modifying prescribed work procedures and by setting output quotas.

One of the Hawthorne experiments, the so-called bank-wiring observation room, illustrated in detail how the productivity of individual workers could be reduced and standardized by a peer group.

Fourteen men were taken out of their regular department and placed in a separate room to continue their regular work under close observation. Their task was to wire banks of terminals for telephone switchboards. Management set a standard output or "bogey" of 7,200 connections per man per day and offered an elaborate scale of wage incentives to encourage output above the bogey. The operators, more concerned about stretching out the work and avoiding unequal treatment than about maximizing their paychecks, adopted an unstated but effective standard of 6,600 connections per man per day. They arranged matters so that almost all of them were able to report an output close to this figure nearly every day, although to do so required continued adjustment of the pace of work, the transfer of work credit from fast to slow workers, the introduction of a sort of play period in the afternoon, the corruption of the two inspectors assigned to the room, the hoarding of finished work for future contingencies, and considerable tinkering with the count of finished connections. Not all the workers participated in these arrangements, but most of them did. The net effect was that the fastest wiremen completed many fewer connections per day than they were capable of and reported fewer than they actually completed, while the slowest wiremen were given credit for more than they actually produced. Western Electric was, at the time, one of the most "scientifically" managed companies in the country, but the informal arrangements of the wiremen nullified most of the human engineering built into the bank-wiring job. Subsequent studies have detected output quotas enforced by peer-group pressure in hundreds of other factories and in nearly every other kind of large organization—in schools and colleges, in government bureaus and social agencies, hospitals and hotels, even in voluntary associations.

The limitation of output is such a natural response to organizational pressure that the people engaged in it are often unaware of what they are doing, and will deny the existence of an output quota when questioned. If the daily or weekly quota is set so low that even the least competent worker can achieve it without undue effort, it may take no more than a relaxed working pace and frequent coffee breaks to maintain a standardized, uniform level of productivity. If this does not suffice, the methods of the bank wiremen are likely to be called into play; workers who have finished the day's quota may avoid doing more work; work in excess of the quota may be transferred to less competent colleagues or hoarded for another day; breakdowns of machinery or communications can be neatly timed to fill up the unused parts of the work period; and so on. Which method will be favored depends on the nature of the job. For example, visiting nurses and appliance repairmen often develop a masterful technique of stretching out an early afternoon call until it is too late to begin a later call that might last beyond quitting time.

From a supervisor's standpoint, systems of output limitation are not entirely malign. Under some circumstances it is advantageous to be able to count on every worker in a group for a fixed output of uniform quality. In a few occupations, like the building trades, the output quota has become entirely respectable; it is designated as a fair day's work and allows skilled craftsmen to work at predictable cost with very little direct supervision.

What makes output limitation a problem is not that work groups set informal quotas for their daily or weekly output, but that in many instances the quotas are scandalously low. Generally speaking, the more a peer group commands the loyalty of its members, the more uniform will their work be and the less variance among them in output. Rensis Likert, summarizing the evidence from many separate studies in *New Patterns of Management*, showed that strong peer groups committed to the organization's goals are much more productive than weak peer groups in the same organizations.[8] But a strong peer group hostile to management or alienated from the organization's goals is likely to show spectacularly low productivity.

Systematic cheating   The simple limitation of output by peer groups may develop over time into a complicated system of cheating the organization, involving several levels of authority and the active connivance of a large part of the work force. These practices range from relatively innocent rule evasions, like the hoarding of spare parts by shop foremen, to activities that are clearly criminal, like the pilfering of supplies and equipment for outside resale. In one teaching hospital that I studied, interns and nurses customarily borrowed small items from hospital stores and took them home. So many people were involved in this pilferage that it came to seem nearly legitimate and was disregarded by the hospital's administrators even when they knew that, for example, ten thousand clinical thermometers disappeared every year.

The network of collusion required to protect a pattern of cheating may be extensive. In an industrial plant studied by Melville Dalton, shop supervisors were able to hoard spare parts and unauthorized equipment despite frequent surprise inspections ordered by higher management, because the inspectors, in order to maintain the goodwill of their local colleagues, telephoned in advance before each inspection to describe the specific path through the plant that the inspection tour would take.

> Notification that a count was under way provoked a flurry among executives to hide some of the parts. Motor and hand trucks with laborers and skilled workers who could be spared were assembled in a given department. Then, materials not to be counted were moved to: (1) little known and inaccessible spots in the plant; (2) basements and pits that were dirty and therefore unlikely to be examined; (3) departments that had already been inspected but could be approached circuitously while the counters were en route between the official storage areas; and (4) areas where other materials and supplies might be used as a camouflage for parts.[9]

Dalton comments that cooperation among shop supervisors to use each other's hiding places and to move men and materials from one shop to another during these exercises were notably smoother than their cooperation in carrying out official activities.

A frightening example of systematic cheating that implicated an entire work force in a pattern of criminal activity comes from a study by Joseph Bensman and Israel Gerver of a factory producing wing assemblies for air force planes.[10] In that ill-starred establishment, new workers were systematically taught how to use a steel tool called a tap to cut new threads into lock nuts whenever the parts of a wing to be assembled did not line up well enough to be bolted together in the proper way. These tapped connections, of course, would be weaker than the specifications called for and in many cases would conceal a structural defect; unlike connections made in the proper way, they would likely loosen and come apart under vibration in flight.

Understandably, the formal rules of the plant defined taps as criminal instruments. The mere possession of one made a worker subject to instant dismissal—in theory. In practice, as the investigators found, new workers were routinely shown how to use taps and how to conceal their use from plant inspectors, who were nevertheless fully aware that taps were in general use. Foremen not only winked at the practice, but often suggested that workers use a tap to complete a difficult assembly. On occasion they used taps themselves in the presence of workers rather than permit a partly completed assembly to be taken apart and started again. All taps, of course, were privately bought and smuggled into the plant by individual workers, but the official tool crib carried a large supply of tap extractors designed for the sole purpose of extracting taps from the nuts in which they often jammed and broke.

A worker might be severely reprimanded for using a tap by the same foreman who had suggested that he do so, but the reprimand was understood by all concerned to be for his indiscretion in allowing himself to be observed. Actual dismissals for this cause were unknown.

The ultimate responsibility for enforcing the antitap rule did not lie with the plant inspectors, who were peers and close associates of the workers, but with the air force inspectors who had the right to reject defective assemblies. It happened, however, that there were only two air force inspectors for a work force of more than two thousand men. Wherever they went in the plant, the news of their coming went ahead of them. Not only was tapping then temporarily suspended, but workers who were known to be careless about concealing their taps were sent out of the shop until the coast was clear.

There is no automatic check on the extension of a pattern of systematic cheating in a large organization, and as in the case just cited, it can go so far as to undermine the entire work process.

The usual cause of such an extensive breakdown is a gap or barrier of some kind in the organization's line of authority, so that the contaminated operations are effectively insulated from managerial observation or control. This may occur either when top management is physically distant from a given work site and has no local representative with sufficient status to resist informal pressure, as happened in the plant studied by Dalton, or when, as in the air force case just described, the ultimate responsibility for enforcing a rule falls on outsiders who have no effective authority over the organization. Sometimes it happens simply because the social distance between top management and the rank and file is so great that people at the top of the organization cannot observe or control activities on the shop floor, while management's actions, viewed from the bottom of the organization, appear inscrutable or senseless.

It is much easier to prevent the development of systematic cheating in an organization than to cure it once it has developed. Illegitimate practices that have become customary are likely to be defended like legitimate rights. The secretary feels entitled to take office supplies home for her children's schoolwork. The intern regards the free thermometers as a routine perquisite. The foreman cannot imagine operating his shop without a store of parts that do not have to be accounted for.

Where the rot is far advanced, the system of cheating may be so closely intertwined with normal operations that nobody knows how to separate them. The overriding consideration, for the wing-assembly foremen, was that they could not meet their production schedules without permitting the widespread use of taps. The standards built into the production process were unwittingly based on that practice and made no allowance for the expenditure of time, labor, and parts that would have been required to complete each assembly according to its blueprint specifications. It takes a moral Hercules to clean that kind of Augean stable, but the thing can be done, and *is* done innumerable times in the course of human affairs.

Snags in the work flow   The work performed in any organization can be described as a flow of events through time and space. People, equipment, and materials join the work flow at predetermined points and leave it at predetermined points. Whenever an entry is delayed, misplaced, or aborted, the subsequent course of the work flow is disturbed to some extent. The extent of the disturbance varies with circumstances, from a trifling deflection to utter chaos.

It is obvious that an organization's work flow is composed of the work flows of all its component units. Each subsidiary work flow has its own predetermined sequence of events and requires the entry and departure of people, equipment, and materials at predetermined points. At the risk of tediousness, we had better note that each subsidiary work flow is composed in turn of the work flows of *its* components, and so on down the individual worker who, of course, has a work flow of his own. Here, for example, are twelve steps in a classically simple assembly-line task —assembling part of a furnace thermostat[11]:

1. Pick up housing assembly with right hand and transfer it to your left. Turn it so the black-and-white cog is on the left-hand side facing you.

2. Turn large, exposed gear with index finger of left hand until dividing line between black-and-white on cog dial runs up and down with black on the left.

3. Pick up the wheel with right hand while you hold big gear in place with left hand.

4. Assemble time wheel to housing, face out, with 6 P.M. mark on time wheel aligned to mark on housing.

5. Pick up cam shaft screw with right hand. While doing this, turn left hand over so that the back of the housing faces you.

6. Insert cam shaft screw into cam shaft hole with right hand.

7. Place housing upside down in holding fixture with both hands.

8. Pick up two self-tapping screws, one in each hand.

9. Insert screws in two small holes in bearing plate.

10. With screwdriver in right hand, drive all three screws home.

11. Remove housing from fixture with left hand while you dispose of screwdriver with your right hand.

12. Place completed assembly to your left with left hand, handy for the next worker to pick up, while you pick up another housing with your right hand.

This description does not give a specific time for each operation in the sequence, but the time element is implied by a standard, communicated to the worker, of how many gear trains per hour he ought to assemble.

In some other instance, where the timing of successive operations is less self-evident, the entire work flow is controlled by a schedule that specifies the movements of people, equipment, and materials, moment by moment. Here, for example, is part of the banquet manager's schedule for a dinner in honor of a foreign dignitary in a New York Hotel.

1900 hrs.	Velvet rope barriers in position west entrance.
1905	Extra doorman reports for duty to west entrance, head porter, maroon uniform.
1910	4 security guards in position curbside to enforce no standing, no stopping.
1910	Upper-side luggage ramp cleared for TV cameramen; head porter to check cable fitting.
1915	Switchboard to open and hold telephone connection banquet office to west entrance service box and lobby box #3 until royal party clears elevator.
1920	Outer doors locked open unless rain.
1925	P.L. and J.R. arrive curbside.
1928	Operator hold tower elevator ground floor, doors closed.
1930	ETA royal limousine, west entrance, four in party. Contact Captain Nem (red uniform).

1931	Pause on steps for TV.
1933	P.L. and J.R. escort royal party through lobby, with security guards.
1934	Elevator away. P.L. accompany; J.R. notify tower and clear lobby arrangements.

This seems complicated for the simple business of getting four people out of a car, up a few steps, and down a short corridor to a waiting elevator, but it is perfectly normal for any event of a public character to be prescheduled to this extent in order to protect the participants against the effects of Murphy's famous law.

The snags that may develop in organizational work flows are too numerous to catalog. In the instance above, for example, the royal limousine arrived on time, but at the *north* entrance of the hotel, so that the TV cameramen did not get any pictures and the banquet manager did not catch up with the party until they had been on the tower floor for some time.

The problems created for an alert and well-tuned organization when plans go awry in this way seem desperate, but are not very serious. The serious snags that appear in organizational work flows are more chronic, being ingrained in individual habits and group practices. They are difficult to remove. Among the common snags are useless work, unsynchronized fluctuations of workload, and irrational priorities.

Useless work occurs in every organization, but it is particularly characteristic of white-collar operations, especially those that have been running a long time. Its emblem is the sextuplicate invoice: copy one becomes the basis for charging, copy two accompanies the order, copy three serves as a notice to the recipient, copies four five, and six, are routed in various directions through various offices, reprocessed, and eventually filed without the slightest useful effect.

Red tape has more of a vegetable than a mechanical character, and its luxuriant growth can only be kept in check by periodic, drastic pruning. The connoisseur of red tape can easily find sequences of paper work in any large organization that require elaborate forms to be filled out, collated, collected, combined, and distributed without being read by anybody. These forms are eventually put in a file that nobody ever consults, without having contributed to the organization's purposes in any way. A variant form of useless paper work is the application of expensive cost-saving or cost-monitoring procedures to transactions too small to support them, as, for example, when the paper work required by a small maintenance job costs four or five times as much as the job itself. Government agencies are particularly susceptible to this problem because of the pressure that is always associated with accounting for public funds.

Unsynchronized fluctuations of workload are particularly characteristic of assembly lines and other productive operations more or less similar to assembly lines in that partly finished materials move from one department to another while undergoing a sequence of irreversible operations that must be performed in a set order.

Adjusting the rate of work in any given department to the rates of work up and down the line is, of course, a continuous problem, since whenever the work of one department is slowed by breakdowns, absences, or a shortage of some necessary item, departments down the line are forced to slow up and wait because they lack work, and departments up the line are tempted to slow down to prevent finished work from piling up. How often these slowdowns occur and how heavily they affect production depends in part on external conditions, like the seasonality of supply for raw materials, and in part on the design of the assembly line or line process. A well-designed production line has a sufficient number of shunts and alternatives to absorb routine fluctuations in the output of its sections. Poorly designed production lines run at reduced capacity most of the time while their managers blame the weather or the union.

As a matter of fact, an ill-designed line may adapt as poorly to improvements of productivity as to work stoppages. William Whyte reports a sad little experiment in a toy factory, where a group of eight girls sat in a straight line spray-painting toys that passed them on moving hooks. They complained that the hooks moved by them too quickly, and to meet this complaint, the foreman reluctantly installed a speed control that enabled the girls to adjust the speed themselves. As so often happens in this kind of experiment, the average speed reached by these workers when they were allowed to set their own variable pace was considerably above the constant speed about which they had previously complained. But the story had an unhappy ending:

> Within three weeks the girls were operating 30 per cent to 50 per cent above what was expected for their training time, with the result that they were earning more than many skilled workers in the plant. The increased production of the paint room caused an excess of toys in the next process and a deficit of toys coming into the paint room. This caused so much dissension among the workers in other parts of the plant that the superintendent arbitrarily revoked the learning bonus and returned the hooks to the old time-studied, constant speed. Production dropped and within a short time, the foreman and all but two girls had quit.[12]

Some types of enterprise, like canneries, are inherently susceptible to gluts and deficits of raw material as well as to work stoppages because of weather and other seasonal factors. Steel mills, refineries, and computer-controlled operations in general are particularly vulnerable to stoppage because the cost of starting up after a shutdown is extremely high in relation to the cost of routine operation.

The design of production lines that can absorb and adjust to normal fluctuations in the productivity of their component sections is accomplished by means of operations research, which may be conducted either formally—with heavy reliance on mathematical formulas and computer simulations—or informally—with pencil and paper and lots of arithmetic. In either case, the object of operations research is to achieve control and flexibility by counting and measuring all of the elements involved in the production process and getting a sure grip on the numerical relationships among them. The concept is applicable not only to assembly lines and other obvious examples of linear work flow; it can also be used to improve the meshing of parts in a school system, a newspaper, an airline, a library, or indeed in any other type of large establishment where complex, repetitive work is undertaken.

Irrational priorities are characteristic of organizations of every type that have well-developed social structures and active networks of informal communication. In such organizations, rational priorities springing from the technical requirements of the work process are often overborne by the claims of status and the obligations of friendship.

The problem can be observed in the nearest convenient factory (or hospital, university, railroad, or boatyard) in which departments depend to some extent on centralized maintenance facilities—electricians, carpenters, painters, steam fitters, machinists—to keep their equipment in good working order. All departments will claim as high a priority as they can for their own maintenance jobs, on the basis of technical necessity. If department heads requesting maintenance work are allowed or compelled to distinguish between routine and urgent jobs, perhaps by a system of tags, nearly every job will carry an "urgent" tag, experience having shown that jobs tagged as "routine" never reach the head of the waiting line.

A closer study of the situation will almost invariably show that some departments receive consistent favorable treatment and that other departments are consistently discriminated against in getting maintenance work done, and that these outcomes cannot be explained by the relative urgency of their maintenance problems but are affected by the informal status of the department head, his personal relationships with the maintenance foremen, and a variety of other factors that are more social than technical. To the extent that this occurs—and it always seems to occur to some extent—production necessarily suffers, since the jobs that are done first are not those most needed to get the work out.[13]

PROBLEMS OF QUALITY CONTROL

When a snag appears in a work process, the workers who cope with it often have a choice between allowing the volume of production to decline or allowing the quality of the product to deteriorate while keeping the volume of production close to its planned level. This is not always a clean, sharp choice, since varying degrees of compromise are possible, but it is a real choice nonetheless and is made nearly every day in nearly every organization as snags develop. Many large organizations are heavily dependent on numerical measures of output to coordinate the flow of work among departments, and they try to hold department heads to their production quotas, regardless of circumstances. Measures of quality are much more elusive and indefinite than measures of quality, and a deterioration of quality is generally harder to detect than a shortfall in the number of units produced or the number of services performed. Under these conditions, there is a built-in tendency for product quality to deteriorate while production quotas are ostensibly met. When the decay of quality is sufficiently advanced, both managers and workers find themselves entangled in a sticky web of collusive and shoddy practices, as we saw in the case of the wing-assembly plant, which met its production quota by manufacturing unsafe airplane parts.

On a much larger scale, the sacrifice of quality to quantity has been one of the major obstacles to economic progress in the Soviet Union, where the whole unlimited power of the state pushes the factory or farm manager to meet his production quota, while the Central Planning Authority is too remote from the work site to exercise any vestige of effective quality control. Joseph Berliner relates an incident from the history of Soviet agriculture:

> For many years it had been the practice to take the livestock census on January 1. It would seem that January 1 is a rather harmless date; presumably it was selected by an innocent planner with the primary objective of facilitating schedules. However, the collective farms have targets of livestock holdings which they are required to meet, as well as targets of meat deliveries to the State. Ordinarily the peasants would bring their stock for slaughter in the early fall, when they are fattest from the summer grazing. But in order to meet their livestock targets on January 1, they kept their stock through the cold early winter months so that they could be counted in the census. The consequence was a disastrous loss of weight. . . .[14]

In a competitive economy, the consumer's tendency to boycott the manufacturer when a product turns out to be defective—and to tell his friends about it—exerts a moderately effective check on the quality of tangible goods, although it does not prevent careless workmanship or corner-cutting in the concealed parts of a mechanical appliance and gross adulteration of food or chemical products that cannot easily be tested by the consumer. The tendency to sacrifice quality to quantity is especially marked in large-scale enterprises providing services to individuals—hospitals, telephone companies, social agencies, and schools, for example. The consumer has very little bargaining power vis-à-vis these enterprises and few ways of protesting effectively against substandard services, while top management finds it nearly impossible to conduct a continuous surveillance of operations from the consumer's perspective.

The only comfort to be found in a failure of quality control, from the manager's standpoint, is that the workers who are at fault probably have uneasy consciences about it. When a manager sets out to remedy a deterioration in the quality of goods or services produced by his organization, he will find moral allies not only among those who suffer from the deterioration but also among those who are responsible for it.

There are two reliable methods of correcting a systematic failure of quality control in an organization. Sometimes they can be employed separately, but more often they need to be combined. The two methods are (1) the revision of performance criteria to give more weight to measures of quality, and (2) the systematic monitoring of consumer reactions to products and services.

Most organizations are not very responsive to managerial rhetoric ("The primary aim of this Company is service to our Community, our Industry, and our Country"), but they are highly responsive to any definite criterion that is used to assess the performance of individuals and groups. If supervisors are rated according to their ability to fulfill a production quota, with bonuses and promotions going to those who overfulfill their quotas, and reprimands and warnings to those who fall short, most units will fulfill their quotas even if they have to destroy the usefulness of the product or service in order to do so. In Peter Blau's study of a public employment agency—a landmark study of a bureaucracy in action—employment interviewers were at one time rated by the number of interviews they completed, and during that era they interviewed a great many job applicants but found jobs for relatively few of them. At another time they were rated according to the proportion of interviews that resulted in job placements. Now they interviewed too few applicants but found jobs for most of them. And so on through a series of changes in the criteria of performance, each change eliciting a reaction that was clearly rational from the standpoint of the interviewer, although not necessarily advantageous for their clients.[15]

Measures of quality, by their nature, are more difficult to make and somewhat more susceptible to error than simple counts of the quantity of goods produced or services performed. But in the typical case, the difficulty is not overwhelming, and the extra cost of an elaborate system of quality control is one of the most profitable investments an organization can make.

Another method is to monitor the quality of products and services from the standpoint of the ultimate or intermediate consumers who are more directly affected by fluctuations of quality, but whose reactions are ordinarily concealed from the manager by differences of interest and perspective as well as by the screens deliberately erected by subordinates.

Of the various types of informal social research useful in the management of organizations, consumer research is perhaps the easiest and the most informative. For example, pharmaceutical manufacturers' studies of the attitudes and practices of physicians with regard to particular ethical (prescription) drugs have invariably shown substantial discrepancies between the manufacturer's view of a product and the physician's. A drug conceived by the manufacturer as a powerful analgesic and a substitute for morphine is prescribed by physicians as a substitute for aspirin. An anoretic (appetite-reducing) product designed by the manufacturer for the treatment of mildly overweight patients is found by a survey to be used exclusively in the treatment of extremely obese patients requiring weight reductions of a hundred pounds or so. A special iron-rich milk formula to feed anemic infants is unused for that purpose, but a small number of pediatricians prescribe it for all the normal infants under their care.

When physicians using any of these products are asked to specify the side effects that concern them in prescribing a given product, the list of side effects they give invariably differs from the manufacturer's list of expected side effects, both in saliency and distribution.

When the reactions of patients to the same products are surveyed in a similar fashion (by interviewing a randomly selected cross section of the patients treated), the patient's view of each product, his estimate of its clinical effectiveness, and his perception of its advantages and drawbacks are spectacularly different from those of either the manufacturer or the physician. The pain reliever previously mentioned is identified as a narcotic by many patients and they avoid taking it continuously for fear of becoming addicted. Patients identified the anoretic drug by its unpleasant aftertaste, of which the manufacturer and the physician are scarcely aware. When it was prescribed, the patient obediently bought it but seldom took it for more than a day or two, so that the effectiveness physicians reported in the treatment of extremely obese patients was illusory.

Such consumer research does not, of course, provide immediate solutions to problems of product quality, but it does give the manager of a producing organization a more realistic picture of the attributes of his products than he can possibly obtain by his own unaided observations, and thereby lays the foundation for a higher level of quality control.

CHOOSING THE RIGHT EQUIPMENT

My friend Richter, the entomologist, lived for a long time in the upper Amazon jungle in an Indian village where the livelihood of the people was largely dependent on the canoes they built for fishing and local travel during the dry season. The rainy season in that region is so extremely humid that no man-made object escapes decay for very long. There are no caves or natural shelters in which to preserve objects, and there is no way of making permanent records. Nevertheless, an elaborate technique of canoe-building is transmitted from generation to generation. The way it is done, according to Richter, is that every canoe is built cooperatively by six to eight active men while a group of elders standing at the edge of the worksite describe in chorus the traditional work sequence taking place under their eyes, and, on the other side of the clearing, a group of adolescent boys repeat everything they say. Meanwhile the workers in between them silently match their actions to the customary words.

"Now the third boat-builder picks up the long adze," chant the elders.

"Now the third boat-builder has picked up the long adze," the boys repeat.

"Now the third boat-builder strikes the front end of the big log with a raking motion," sing the elders.

"The third boat-builder is striking the front end of the big log with a raking motion," the boys repeat, as the third boat-builder does so.

In such a traditional society, the selection of the appropriate equipment for a particular purpose is no problem at all. There is only one technology available. The equipment it requires does not allow substitution. The results that can be achieved when the traditional work sequence is carefully followed are known to everyone in advance.

Our technology is, of course, much more efficacious and versatile, but for that very reason the selection of suitable equipment for a given task may present quite a difficult problem.

The mention of technology suggests large-scale industry, but in fact there are technological problems in every type of organization. To illustrate the point, let us take our examples from a church.

Nearly every church has bells in its steeple and an organ in its choir. These are durable items of equipment, but sooner or later they require major repair or replacement; and when they do, the modern congregation has an interesting range of alternatives—bells rung by hand ropes, bells mechanically struck, electronically controlled bells, or a carillon that rings convincingly without any bells at all. It is also possible to devise hybrid systems, such as one in which relatively small bells are rung by hand ropes but electronically amplified.

The selection of an organ involves a similarly wide choice. A few churches might still consider a new organ pumped by hand or foot, but the usual choices are whether to buy a pneumatically operated model with a full-size set of pipes, or to install a small set of pipes with electronic amplification, or to go to a fully automated console that produces organ sounds without any vibrating columns of air.

The decision is not easy. The cost of a carillon or an organ is very high in relation to the resources of the average congregation, and an error in selection is almost irretrievable. Whoever does the selecting must balance the somewhat lower cost of the electronically operated instrument against the greater reliability and lesser service requirements of mechanically operated equipment. But this is not an easy calculation to make, since, on the one hand, the replacement of parts is generally simpler with an electronic instrument, but, on the other hand, the dependence on a particular supplier is much greater. The comparative frequency of breakdowns, which might be the decisive factor, is nearly impossible for a nonexpert to discover in advance.

Under these circumstances, even the most careful and judicious process of selection is likely to miscarry. The best rule of thumb is to refuse any equipment whose long-term workability cannot be demonstrated in one way or another by independent evidence.

The selection of a new carillon or organ also involves a standard sociological problem. It is obviously unwise to make those selections without the full participation of the bell ringer and the organist, but what is not so obvious is that the selection ought not to be determined solely by their preferences, since it is very likely that their preferences will not be pure professional judgments. Some preferences will be based on past experience—the organist who has struggled with badly designed amplifiers may be unwilling to consider the possibility that other amplifiers work well; some have to do with the conservation of status—the bell ringer who knows how to ring difficult changes does not look kindly upon the keyboard carillon that makes his skill obsolete; some reflect ulterior motives—the organist reckons that the rewiring required by one type of hybrid organ will enable her to install an electric heater under her bench. Whoever is ultimately responsible for the purchasing decision must walk a fine line, taking account of the operator's knowledge and experience while disregarding the operator's prejudices. The situation calls for gathering as much information as can reasonably be obtained and reaching a collective rather than an individual decision.

If it is any comfort to the committee of vestrymen, the same problem arises in much larger organizations—in selecting jet airliners, steam turbines, and nuclear generators, for example.

The proper equipment for a particular organizational task will generally be located somewhere between the crudest possible equipment, which is clumsy, time-consuming, accessible, and probably reliable, and the most sophisticated equipment available, which is expensive, difficult to install and maintain, and possibly not warranted by the volume or character of work to be done.

The manager ultimately responsible for the selection of

equipment must be prepared to resist two opposing kinds of pressure from the operators of the equipment and their supervisors: on the one hand, a sort of Luddite resistance to the spinning machine that replaces the skillful fingers of the artisan; on the other hand— and much more prevalent nowadays—a craving for the shiny new machine with intricate dials that takes no account of relative costs and benefits. In approving the replacement of old by new equipment, the manager ought to be as deaf as possible to both sorts of appeal and base his decision on the coolest calculation of which he is capable.

How to recognize high productivity

The yardsticks by which an organization's performance is measured vary according to the type of organization, but a manager can be reasonably satisfied if he observes that:

1. There is general agreement within the organization about how to measure its productivity.

2. The measurements used are sufficiently sensitive that fluctuations in efficiency and effectiveness can be detected almost immediately.

3. Most of the people he directly supervises do their work to his satisfaction.

4. Most of the groups he indirectly supervises turn out the volume and quality of work demanded from them.

5. He often finds it difficult to devise a reward commensurate with the outstanding performance of an individual or group.

6. The reorganization of an ineffective unit is not likely to provoke resistance from other parts of the organization.

7. Operating reports are customarily accurate and reliable. Systematic misreporting would not be tolerated anywhere in the organization.

8. When projections of future output are made, the actual output achieved is as likely to exceed the projection as to fall short.

9. An increase in output does not normally induce a deterioration of quality.

10. The organization is imitated by its competitors more than it imitates them.

11. Where output limitation is practiced within the organization, the limits are set fairly high.

12. There is no evidence of cheating, vandalism, or sabotage in the work process.

13. Rank-and-file members of the organization take the quality of its performance as seriously as high-ranking members.

14. Most breakdowns in the work flow are repaired without the intervention of management.

15. There is relatively little resistance to technological improvement if the persons concerned are consulted in advance.

4:Morale

You have lost your subject when you have lost his inclination; you are to preside over the minds, not the bodies of men. The soul is the essence of a man; and you cannot have the true man against his inclination.

SIR WALTER RALEIGH TO A YOUNG PRINCE

Morale and happiness

The morale of an organization should not be confused with the happiness of the individuals who belong to it. Morale is *satisfaction with an organization,* not with life in general. An organization has high morale when most of its members: (1) accept its goals; (2) obey its important rules; and (3) continue to participate in its program. Generally speaking, these conditions are favorable to the happiness of the participating individuals, but there are some significant exceptions. High morale without happiness is characteristic of organizations that cope with extreme stress under strong leadership. The castaways of the *Bounty* mutiny, sailing their overcrowded, open boat three thousand miles across an empty sea under the strict command of Captain Bligh, seem to have developed a very high level of morale, although they were not happy during their painful voyage.

Conversely, individuals who profit from the collapse of an organization's morale may be quite happy, like the Japanese corporal who, during the disintegration of the Japanese forces in New Britain during World War II, managed to enslave two of his officers and put them to work in a vegetable patch.

Under normal circumstances, being part of a high-morale group is a much more pleasant experience than being part of a low-morale group engaged in the same activity, so that in general high morale contributes to individual happiness. On the other hand, it is not the only source of individual happiness, nor is it necessarily more gratifying than alternative pleasures. The soldier who marches off to battle with his high-morale regiment might have been happier staying at home with his girl.

There is another important difference between morale and happiness. In most organizations, morale is correlated with rank. The higher the rank, the higher the morale, if only because the leaders of an organization have a larger stake in the success or failure of its program and identify more closely with it. But happiness is not subject to the same effect. It tends to be an inverse function of age, the younger members of the organization generally reporting themselves as happier than their elders.

The most important distinction between morale and happiness, from the manager's standpoint, is that while he has no way of keeping all the people in his organization happy, he has, or can acquire, the means to sustain a high level of morale.

These means consist of policies about recruiting, training, and evaluating people; policies about rewarding and punishing people; decisions taken under these policies; and procedures for the peaceful settlement of the conflicts they inevitably provoke. We shall first consider each type of personnel policy separately and then attend to some of their joint consequences.

Recruiting

Organizations, even of the same type, differ greatly in turnover rates and therefore in the amount of managerial time and effort that must be devoted to recruitment. Many American companies have a curiously hybrid system, turnover being very high for blue-collar employees and very low for white-collar employees. In one large manufacturing company I studied some years ago, the median seniority of shopworkers was barely seven months, the median seniority of office workers was around six years, and that of executives, fourteen years. In a Dutch plant in the same industry at the same time, the median seniority was sixteen years for male employees at all levels but only three years for female employees, who customarily left the company when they married.

Other types of organizations show similar variability. The famous Bach Choir at Bethlehem, where some singers remain continuously on the roster for half a century, has an annual turnover rate of around 10 percent, while other well-known choirs replace most of their members from one season to the next.

Whenever turnover is high, the manager of an organization will spend a large part of his time in recruitment and can anticipate that the success or failure of his administration will be expressed, to a large extent, by recruitment results. When turnover is low, recruitment will take less time but will be no less significant for morale, since long-service members will be extremely sensitive to any trends they can read out of the characteristics of the few people recruited, such as a decline of the organization's drawing power or a threatened shift from amateur to professional singers.

There is a nearly universal tendency to underestimate the average turnover rate in an organization that has a variable turnover rate, so that participants are surprised by the rapidity of change in the human landscape around them. The manager who concerns himself closely with the recruitment process may be able to mold an organization to a new image by the cumulative effect of routine personnel decisions more quickly than by direct reorganization.

Even when no such result is desired, the recruitment process offers extraordinary opportunities to the manager who wants to improve an organization. Most organizations do not select their new members in a wholly rational way, yet this is one of the sectors of organizational activity most amenable to a rational approach. The objectives of a rational recruitment policy are first, to locate and attract as many well-qualified recruits as one needs; second, to maintain or raise the total value of the organization's human assets; third, to minimize the cost incurred by the recruitment process when unsuitable persons are selected or when recruitment has adverse effects on the morale of people already in place.

There is little superficial resemblance between the curbside hiring of a casual laborer to help unload a truck and the worldwide search for a distinguished conductor to take charge of a major symphony orchestra. Nevertheless, there are certain broad principles that cover both cases.

Let us consider how a manager who has an important position to fill ought to go about it. We assume that a decision has already been made to seek a candidate outside the organization, either because no insider is suitably qualified or for some other good reason. Note in passing that no wheel should turn in the recruitment process before that decision is made. To place insiders in competition with outsiders for a position is always a mistake and easily turns into a catastrophe. It almost automatically undermines the loyalty of the inside candidates, even if one of them is ultimately appointed over the outside competition. By contrast, a decision to recruit from outside may be resented when there are suitably qualified inside candidates, but is unlikely to have serious repercussions, provided none of the inside candidates has been promised, or thinks he has been promised, the position. Where there are several qualified insiders, each of them will normally regard the appointment of an outsider as a lesser evil than losing the contest to a colleague.

The optimum procedure for recruiting an outsider is simple and straightforward, although moderately difficult to follow in real life.

1. *Determine in advance what qualifications are essential.* The unspoken corollary to this rule is to exclude and ignore all nonessential qualifications.

Let us suppose that as the director of an art museum you are looking for a new secretary and a new curator of sculpture.

The essential qualifications for the secretarial position are a high order of typing skill, competence in general office work, and a personality agreeable to the immediate supervisor, yourself. These qualifications can be established by tests, references, and an interview; no special clairvoyance is required to make a rational choice provided that you are willing to exclude such nonessential qualifications as age, beauty, race, ethnicity, class origin, formal education, and familiarity with the art world. To the extent that you take these factors into account, after determining them to be nonessential, you unreasonably restrict the pool of applicants and diminish your chance of making a good selection. The best candidate may be a young man with a degree in English literature or a middle-aged high school dropout from a hospital office.

The essential qualifications for the curator of sculpture are, let us say, a degree in art history, some competence in restoration, and previous successful experience as a gallery manager. It does not matter much whether his gallery experience involved sculpture, and it should not matter at all whether he is married or divorced, male or female, white, black, red, or yellow; Protestant, Catholic, Jew, or Christian Scientist; chaste or lecherous, athletic or puny. His appearance doesn't matter, and so far as is humanly possible, you should pay no attention to the attractiveness of his personality.

Should age be taken into account? That depends upon whether you want a curator of sculpture who will hold that position indefinitely or one who will use it as a springboard for promotion. In the first instance, forty might be a reasonable minimum age; in the second instance, forty might be an appropriate maximum.

One other qualification is necessarily essential for the curator of sculpture. Since the position involves the custody of valuable property and occasional opportunities for large-scale fraud, an absolutely clean record with respect to honesty and trustworthiness ought to be required. But beware of unsupported inferences; there is no reason to assume that a homosexual or a habitual traffic offender is inclined to dishonesty.

To focus on essential qualifications and ignore the candidate's other traits calls for a surprising amount of moral fiber. Particularly when a position is much sought after, it is hard not to be ruled by the spurious claims of attractiveness, ethnicity, and compatibility, and the practice of the rule is further hampered by the fact that for some positions, attractiveness, ethnicity, and compatibility *are* essential qualifications.

2. *Consider as few candidates as possible.* Every offer of a position, paid or unpaid, professional or volunteer, important or insignificant, tests a tiny sector of the labor market. If the offer turns up no applicants at all, it signifies either that the requirements have been set too high or the rewards of the position have been set too low, which are alternate ways of saying the same thing. In that event, it is necessary to enlarge the scope of the search by advertising or other means, and if that doesn't work, to improve the offer. By contrast, the appearance of a host of applicants in response to an offer suggests that the qualifications for the position have been set too low or the rewards too high. The best resolution of this awkward situation is to raise the qualifications informally so that nearly all of the applicants are screened out and only a few remain to be considered.

There are several reasons why it is better to consider a few candidates, rather than many, and preferably one at a time, making a final decision on each one before moving on to the next. The whole aim of a rational recruitment process is to get each candidate into sharp focus so that the people making the appointment can visualize accurately how he would fit into the new position. This sort of visualization is much easier to do for one candidate, whose history and characteristics can be considered at leisure, than for two or three, and is nearly impossible with a larger number.

The availability of an excessive number of qualified applicants will often tempt the recruiter into a search for the "best possible candidate." This is always and necessarily a wild-goose chase; people are not really comparable to that extent, and potential behavior is never predictable with so much accuracy. Any serious effort to locate the best possible candidate is likely to turn up an overqualified candidate instead; that is, someone who is too good for this particular position and who will discover that for himself before he has occupied it very long.

Comparing candidates with each other rather than with the position to be filled induces all sorts of distortions into the recruiter's perspective, and when collective judgments are made, any existing factions in the organization are sure to seize upon this ready-made opportunity for a fight. The consideration of one candidate at a time works better. If several qualified candidates are available, they should be placed in rank order of apparent desirability by any reasonable method and then considered in order one at a time, each name being definitely rejected before the next on the list is taken up. If the people involved in the selection are unwilling to deprive themselves of the excitement of a contest—as they often are—the next best thing is to consider only two or three names at a time. Above that number, the selection process becomes chaotic and its outcome will probably be determined by accident.

3. *Make sure that the candidate understands the position.* It is by violation of this rule that recruitment most often goes wrong. Both large and small organizations very frequently misinform the people they recruit as to the duties, status, and opportunities attached to their prospective positions. Out of eagerness and over-enthusiasm, they may tell a few little lies. Of all the world's little white lies, those told to a candidate during the recruitment process are the least likely to be forgotten. They provide him with a foundation for a whole structure of future grievances.

In order to describe a position to a candidate you must make sure that (1) you understand the position yourself, and (2) other people share your understanding of it. If you try to do this carefully and systematically at the beginning of the recruitment process, you may discover that there is more ambiguity than you supposed in the position and that the personal characteristics of the last incumbent are perhaps deluding everyone into expecting too much—or too little—of the next incumbent. The resolution of these ambiguities to the point where the obligatio1s and rewards of each position can be clearly explained to a candidate will do more to simplify recruitment than anything else.

4. *Study the candidate.* Years ago, Reece McGee and I made an intensive study of how major universities selected new professors from among outside candidates. One of the findings of the study was that a faculty candidate's publications were the most important part of his record. But almost invariably, the people involved in the recruitment process omitted to read the candidate's books and papers in the course of evaluating him. With a kind of sociable laziness, they traded unfounded impressions with colleagues who had also failed to look at the evidence, instead of buckling down to long hours of rather tedious reading.

Considering any outside candidate for an organizational position, we have recourse to five basic kinds of information:

1. Biographical facts—generally presented by the applicant during the interview or in a written application, occasionally provided by third parties.

2. Official records—documentary evidence of the candidate's identity, birth, religion, mental status, schooling, citizenship, and professional certification, among other things.

3. Aptitudes and abilities—as demonstrated by many kinds of tests and evaluations, some obviously valid, like a test of typing speed; some rather doubtful, like an inventory of personality traits.

4. References—testimonials about the candidate's competence and character by trustworthy persons who know him better than we do.

5. The candidate's attitude toward the organizational program—generally deduced from his behavior during an interview.

The organization rather than the candidate usually decides what specific information is to be presented in each of these categories. Every field and every organization has arbitrary conventions of its own. Applicants to a law school are often required to present character references from ministers and respectable neighbors; applicants to a graduate school of arts and sciences are required to present references from former teachers but from no one else. Candidates for the British Foreign Service were formerly required to take an advanced test in literature, including the composition of original Greek verse. American corporations commonly require an executive candidate to submit to a series of personality tests intended to reveal the profile of his subconscious mind. Some organizations select candidates largely on the basis of their response to a critical question or incident. One firm of British merchant bankers asked every candidate, in the course of an otherwise innocuous interview, the following critical question, "If you were today given, or inherited, an income which would be completely adequate to permit you to live exactly in the way you wanted, and to do just what you wanted, what would you do?"[1] The only acceptable answer was something like, "I would bring the money into merchant banking and make more."

Even when a critical question is used to make the final decision, there is a great deal of preliminary information about the candidate and his qualifications to be sifted through first, and this is where most organizations, in my observation, do a sloppy and careless job. References, as every schoolboy knows, need to be verified. Few people bother. A telephone conversation is infinitely more informative than a letter of reference, but few people trouble to pick up the phone, even when important positions are involved, and fewer still have prepared the questions they want to ask. To the professors who don't read the candidate's books, we must add the shop managers who don't ask for a sample of his machine work, the architect's clients who don't bother to look at what he has previously built, and the churches that don't send anyone to hear the new minister preach. It is commonplace for organizations to require an applicant to fill out a long life-history form full of prying and inquisitive questions, but to fail to verify in any way that the applicant has given his true name and address.

5. *Don't shilly-shally.* Neither the organization involved in the recruitment process nor the individuals caught up in it have anything to gain from dragging it out, yet that happens surprisingly often, usually because the organization's procedure is defective in some of the ways we have been discussing. The attempt to consider a large number of candidates simultaneously, for example, may lead to an impasse in which no candidate appears acceptable. The failure to describe a position clearly often leads to a situation in which the organization and the candidate haggle wearily back and forth until somebody's patience runs out. Inattention to the evidence is likely to lead to a standoff between competing candidates, backed by evenly matched factions.

Most of these awkward outcomes can be avoided if the manager responsible for the recruitment process resolves never to accept a doubtful candidate except in an absolute emergency, and never to delay the appointment of a satisfactory candidate in the bleary hope that a better one will come along. While the search for a suitable incumbent will necessarily be long when a position is particularly difficult to fill, the organization's dialogue with any one candidate ought to be relatively brief and decisive. Nothing whatever is gained by keeping an ultimately unsuccessful candidate on the string for a long time. Much can be lost by doing the same to an ultimately successful candidate who then enters the organization without enthusiasm and without any sense of being wanted and chosen.

Training

The various things done by organizations to assure that candidates for positions turn into successful incumbents are generally lumped together under the name of training. The term is misleading because it suggests a process whereby the trainee gradually learns to do exactly what the trainer wants him to do, as in the training of circus animals. In fact, the training of organizational recruits is a very different kind of process, and its final outcome generally represents a compromise between the plans of the trainer and the preferences of the trainee, further modified by all the accidents they encounter during the training period. Nevertheless, training is the term in use and we will follow it respectfully even when it leads to peculiar forms of statement, as in a recent textbook of industrial psychology, which has a chapter on "Training in Self-Knowledge."

In order for a recruit to become the successful incumbent of an organizational position, he must acquire not only the specific skills the position calls for but also a new image of himself and of the organization, a new set of social relationships, and a new code of moral values. The recruit who comes from outside the organization has a great deal more to learn than the recruit transferred or promoted from within the organization, but he has also the advantage of starting with a clean slate, while the inside recruit is called upon to change his map of a familiar territory and to abandon old friends and familiar ideas. This is a painful process and it often ends in frustration or failure. The recruit from outside, of course, may have similar problems if he comes from another organization of the same type in which everything was done a little differently.

In the vast majority of organizations—large and small, public and private, commercial and voluntary—the importance of training is underestimated and training procedures are less than adequate, with the result that many promising recruits leave the organization soon after they join it and the usefulness of many others is permanently reduced by a clumsy initiation. Indeed, it is easy to find organizations or segments of organizations in which nobody has been properly trained. I know of an office building with a large staff of janitors, none of whom have ever learned the right way to mop a floor or sweep a staircase. A recent study of a pediatric clinic disclosed that all of its resident physicians made the same elementary mistakes in attempting to communicate with the mothers of the infants brought to them for treatment.[2] In university teaching, it is a scandal of long standing that the inexperienced new faculty member receives no training in the difficult art of classroom teaching; he is expected to acquire it by instinct, which often fails, or by trial and error, which is hard on his students.

The reasons so many organizations neglect training are understandable. The trainee must be supported while he produces relatively little. The organization may not be able to suspend the normal operations associated with the trainee's position while it waits for him to be properly trained. The cost of scanted training may be great, but, spread over a long period of time, it is inconspicuous. And to confuse the issue, there are always a few people who seem to do very well without training.

Because the importance of training is so commonly underestimated, the manager who wants to make a dramatic improvement in organizational effectiveness without challenging the status quo will find a training program a good place to start. With normal turnover, it may not be long before the alumni of his training program have changed the status quo beyond recognition.

Successful training, we said, involves the acquistion of new skills, new images of self and organization, a new set of social relationships, and a new code of moral values—all of which involve quite different kinds of learning. An adequate training program must rely on a variety of learning methods and a variety of agents within the organization, including fellow trainees.

There are always new skills to be learned in a new position, even when the recruit is highly skilled to begin with. The organization knows, or can discover, just how it wants the task performed, and the recruit can learn to do it that way if the trainer gets to him soon enough and stays with him long enough, and if he is given the opportunity and time to practice the desired technique until it becomes a habit. Nine times out of ten it doesn't work out that way. The trainee is allowed to develop his own technique by trial and error, or by imitating others, before the trainer gets to him, and will then defend it to the death. Or the training begins in time but is superficial. The technique is shown to the trainee without sufficient explanation or without a sufficient opportunity for super-vised practice, so that he eventually improvises a technique of his own which is an imperfect copy of the desired technique and to which, again, he becomes firmly attached.

Training, in sum, must be very patient if it is to be successful. Undue haste undoes the whole effort.

With respect to the new image of his own role and of the whole organization that the trainee must have to function effec-tively in his new position, these must develop in the course of his own experience—they cannot be imprinted on his consciousness from outside or above. But if these subjective images are to mesh reasonably well with the images held by others, and with external reality, the organization must provide the trainee with a tremen-dous volume of information, much more than he typically thinks he wants, and very much more than he would pick up unaided.

There is a kind of optical illusion whereby everyone from the top to the bottom of an organization is deluded into thinking that his own picture of the organization shows it as it really is. Because of this illusion, it is difficult for a manager, or any other experi-enced member of an organization, to visualize it through the eyes of a newly joined recruit or vice versa. The opportunities for mu-tual misunderstanding are endless.

We discussed in the previous chapter some of the things a manager might do to fill in the blank spots and correct the errors in his own image of the organization. What concerns us here is how he can provide the new incumbent of a position with an adequate map of the territory he has just entered.

In the second chapter, I mentioned the air force division in which a majority of officers were unfamiliar with the official mis-sion of their own units, and many were uncertain about who re-ported to them and who they reported to. Many of the enlisted men did not recognize the name of the unit to which they were assigned, or their own job assignments, or the positions of various persons from whom they received orders.

Similar states of misorientation can easily be found in civilian enterprises of all kinds and even in voluntary associations. I discovered recently, for example, that most of the members of the governing board of a mental health association could not tell whether the association was an arm of the federal government, of the state government, or not of any government at all, and that they did not agree about its primary function.

Organizations in this condition are of necessity ineffective, and their members almost invariably have low morale because of the difficulties they experience in carrying out duties and pursuing goals they do not understand.

Orientation to an organization is a long-term matter. It takes years to learn the ins and outs of an established organization and constant study to keep up with its shifts and changes. Research evidence suggests that orientation to a large organization may reach a maximum in ten years or more and thereafter gradually decline.

Just as the recruit who has no opportunity to learn the correct technique for performing an organizational task is sure to develop an improvised technique of his own that he may later refuse to give up, so the recruit who is not given a full, accurate picture of the organizational structure and his place in it will invent a distorted picture or acquire one from equally ignorant colleagues and then cling to it with astonishing tenacity. First impressions are as important and lasting in the relationship between an individual and an organization as in the encounter of two individuals. They may be overcome later but are never entirely forgotten.

The manager responsible for bringing new people into an organization must see to it that, at the very beginning, they are given a full, detailed, and intelligible account of how the organization is put together—its structure and program, its long-term goals and operating philosophy, the interrelationship of its units, its history and its plans, and the fullest possible description of the part the recruit is expected to play in the organization's program.

Only part of this information will be absorbed. It needs to be repeated when the dust of the initial encounter between the individual and the organization has cleared and he is beginning to make sense out of the landscape around him, and then should be repeated again and again. No one but the manager responsible for the whole organization is likely to understand the full importance of this orientation, least of all the recruit to whom much of the information will appear hopelessly remote and irrelevant, and who, at best, will absorb only a fraction of it. Nevertheless he needs it, and the organization needs for him to have it.

SOCIALIZING THE RECRUIT

Helping the trainee acquire new skills and new images of himself and the organization are training assignments that take time and effort but do not involve any sociological stress. Helping the trainee to acquire a new set of acquaintances and a new code of moral values are much more chancy training assignments. There is always a possibility that these new acquaintances will be hostile toward the organization's programs and that they will teach the recruit the moral values of an underground opposition.

The classic—and worst—method of inducting a recruit into his new social world is for the trainer to introduce him to a number of his peers and then go away. Not only is the recruit likely to be hazed, in one way or another, but the trainer loses contact with the trainee.

I said this was the worst method, but that appraisal should probably be qualified by the observation that in some traditional organizations it is made to work fairly well by harnessing its defects. In the Coast Guard Academy, when it was studied by Sanford Dornbusch two decades ago,[3] the new cadet or "swab" found himself subject to two inconsistent sets of rules: the regulations and the traditions. The traditions were enforced by peers or upperclassmen. Although they involved prescribed infractions of the regulations, the swab was clearly informed when he entered the academy that he would not suffer for the breaches of regulation he might have to commit in order to obey the traditions. For example, when a swab received demerits for carrying out the hazing orders given by an upperclassman, other upperclassmen contrived to excuse him from official infractions until his demerit account had been balanced. Since Dornbusch's study was made, the elaborate games associated with the hazing system seem to have been abandoned or curtailed in the service academies, partly in an effort to reduce the high attrition rates with which they were associated.

Even if such a system works in a few institutions, most organizations are well advised not to turn over their recruits to an autonomous peer group for socialization. It is best prevented by making sure that repeated personal contact takes place between the trainee and all those superiors whose activities directly affect him, all those people at his own level with whom he ought to be in touch in the course of his routine activities, and of course all of his direct subordinates. People differ greatly in their ability to remember and recall names and faces, so that it is difficult to specify how much working and sociable contact is necessary to introduce a trainee to x number of associates; but it should be more than is usually provided when superficial introductions are made. When the trainee is expected to recognize the fifty people to whom he has been introduced as readily as they recognize him, he is certain to offend some of them before they eventually come into focus. Mechanical devices, like tables of organization with pictures attached, can be very helpful here, but more important is the persistent repetition of occasions for introduction as part of the training program, until real familiarity has been established. These same occasions—whether formal or informal—provide an opportunity for the trainee's organizational superiors to let him know in steadily expanding detail what they expect of him and what they can do for him. This information cannot be conveyed all at once. It has to be communicated bit by bit as the trainee's comprehension of the organization evolves, but it *must* be deliberately communicated. Information acquired by osmosis is certain to be incomplete and inaccurate.

Whether the trainee adopts the code of moral values the organization would like him to have depends in part on how the training is conducted and in part on the moral condition of the organization. The best method of indoctrination is undoubtedly apprenticeship—that ancient system whereby a recruit is trained by an experienced member of the organization who serves as his teacher, supervisor, and model. Apprenticeship has gone out of style in some occupations, but it is still widely practiced wherever people who hold positions of high responsibility are able to select and train their own successors: in the upper reaches of the government and the professions, for example. The apprentice acquires the moral code the organization wants him to have, with all its nuances, by imitating the master. Peer-group resistance to the organization's values is minimized, since apprentices interact more with, and are more influenced by, their masters than their peers.

In a more impersonal training program, the transmission of organizational values to a trainee is relatively simple when those values command full agreement within the organization or within that segment of the organization to which the trainee is exposed. It becomes much more complicated (but not necessarily futile) when there is disagreement.

Organizational values are best transmitted when they are acted out, and not merely announced, by the people responsible for training, or by the people pointed out as models for recruits to follow in the performance of organizational roles. The manager of an organization, who is ex officio a model for recruits, may have an astonishing ability to communicate organizational values in his fleeting contacts with them. That is the age-old secret of successful generalship, and it is applied every day by basketball coaches, tugboat skippers, and certain choirmasters, whose commitment to their roles is so dramatically evident that they strike awe into the recruits who observe them in action.

Another aspect of dramatization is the exaggeration of one or two organizational values. Violations are then represented as wicked and dangerous—in short, as violations of a taboo. I knew a crew coach who so impressed upon his oarsmen the importance of not breaking training that those who ventured to do so generally went to him, confessed, and received an expiatory punishment.

Even in the most humdrum organization, there is likely to be some value that can be exalted. A supermarket, for example, may prefer accuracy at the checkout counter to all other virtues. A police department, although slack in other respects, may be fanatical about the polish and operating condition of patrol cars. Such values are always good for morale even when they involve some loss of efficiency or effectiveness.

Like other forms of drama, the successful inculcation of organizational values calls for a nice blend of truth and artifice. In order for a value to be reliably transmitted to recruits, it must be held with real conviction by the organization's leaders and visibly exemplified in their conduct, but that alone is not sufficient. It must also be presented in an atmosphere of solemnity and excitement, and with the right background music.

Every high-morale organization has ceremonies, although they are not always immediately recognizable to outsiders. (A cocktail party can be as ceremonious as a procession.) It is particularly important from the standpoint of morale that the completion of training be marked by a ceremony that celebrates the recruit's survival through the rigors of training, formalizes his acquisition of a new status, and reminds him of his commitment to the organization's prime values. Such a ceremony is sometimes omitted or scanted because the completion of training appears as a trivial achievement to people already in the organization, but it is the manager's responsibility to see that this singular opportunity for the reinforcement of morale is not wasted.

Here, as a negative example, is the way new employees are introduced to their work in the large furniture store studied by Harry Levenson:

> There is no orientation for new employees. Members of the sales force are given an introductory lecture on company policies and benefits by a member of the personnel department and then shown how to make out a sales slip. They are assigned to a department and turned loose. The department manager is supposed to assign one of the older employees to the newer member to show him around but this is seldom done. The person has to discover on his own where the toilets are, where the cafeteria is, and what time he may take his breaks. Sometimes the outcome is embarrassing. . . . A new employee in the stockroom is given a quick tour by the supervisor to obtain a general impression where the merchandise is located. Then he is on his own. From our observation of the stockroom setting, many new stock people seem to wander for days through the maze of stock before someone takes them in hand and shows them where the merchandise is located.[4]

Evaluating individual performance

The evaluation of the individual's performance in an organization begins with his initial training and continues to his retirement—and sometimes beyond. It is something every organization has to do all the time, although it is nearly impossible to do accurately and well; evaluation always involves errors. Some of these errors destroy the happiness of individuals, while others undermine the organization. There is no way of avoiding errors of evaluation, but something can be done to minimize the damage they cause, as we shall presently see.

The simplest and least troublesome situation is that the trainee or the new incumbent of the position turns out to lack the bare qualifications for his duties. A summer camp hires a bugler who says he is a little rusty but will recover his skill. After three or four days, his bugle calls are still slow and quavering. All we need is another bugler.

It sometimes happens that the new incumbent of an important position shows himself almost at once to be unqualified. I know a college president whose hopeless incompetence was obvious within a month of his inauguration; a half-serious popular book has been written to expound the proposition that people in hierarchies uniformly tend to be promoted beyond their levels of competence. The fully incompetent incumbent of a major position may be difficult or impossible to dislodge, but the problem is not so much to evaluate his performance as to live with it. On the other hand, it is likely that he arrived at his present eminence because of a mistaken evaluation of his performance in the past, or a whole series of mistaken evaluations.

Mistakes in the evaluation of individual performance—not permissible differences of opinion but, rather, downright errors—occur for a variety of reasons and are partly preventable. They come in two styles: favorable evaluations of incompetent performance and unfavorable evaluations of competent performance. But since they have very similar causes, we may as well consider them together.

CAUSES OF MISTAKEN EVALUATIONS

1. *The illusion of consistency.* There is a natural tendency, which seems to be automatically reinforced within organizations, to expect more consistent behavior from other people than our experience with them would predict, and to perceive more consistency in their behavior than they actually display. Nearly every appraisal of an individual's performance in an organizational position is subject to a halo effect produced by this illusion. The indi-

vidual who does one thing conspicuously well or badly is presumed, without evidence, to be meeting his other responsibilities the same way. The individual who was conscientious and hardworking last year is described without hesitation as being conscientious and hardworking this year, even when his conduct has drastically changed.

There is a mountain of evidence from social science research and from history to indicate that inconsistency is normal. Consider, for example, the proofreaders whose performance was studied by C. H. Lawshe and E. D. McGinley.[5] The printing company that employed them proposed three criteria to measure the performance of a proofreader: average output, rate of error, and versatility. Each of these measures was accurate and reliable, but there was no appreciable correlation among them. In other words, a fast proofreader was no more likely to be versatile than a slow proofreader; an accurate proofreader was as likely to be fast as slow, and so on.

Or consider Captain Bligh after he provoked the crew of the *Bounty* to mutiny. He led the sailors who were cast away with him to safety in the longest open boat voyage in the annals of the sea. His inconsistency was habitual: the detailed accounts of that immortal voyage report that while Bligh sustained and inspired his crew at sea, he quarreled dangerously with them whenever they landed on an island. Bligh provoked two other major mutinies before he finally retired as a rear admiral, yet he inspired many subordinates to admiring devotion. How would you rate him as a leader?

Inconsistency of performance over time is so well established that it can be expressed as a kind of statistical law. There have been thousands of studies of the relationship, for example, between high school grades and college grades, between success in job training and success on the job, between conduct in prison and behavior on parole, between vote-getting ability and legislative productivity, as well as innumerable studies relating the achievements of individuals at one time to their achievements at some later time. What all these studies demonstrate is the existence of a "ceiling correlation" of approximately .60 between measures of past performance and measures of future performance. This ceiling is easy to approach with any sensible prediction device or combination of devices, but virtually impossible to exceed. Statistically speaking, a correlation of .60 leaves almost two-thirds of the variance in the future performance unaccounted for.* In plainer language, an individual's past performance tells us something useful about his future performance but does not come anywhere near to predicting it accurately.

2. *The masking of individual performance by a team.* An individual in an organization necessarily belongs to a team, often to several teams at once, and there may be no easy way of disentangling his contributions from those of his teammates or of finding out what his performance would be in another team. In the previous chapter, we saw how a factory peer group operated a system of output limitation that held the output of the most competent workers far below the level of which they were capable and at the same time credited the least competent workers with more output than they actually produced. But even when individual output is unregulated, and when no peer group interposes itself between management and the work process, it is still the case that most members of organizations are engaged in collective tasks in which it is difficult to separate out the effective contribution of an individual, or in which individual output can be measured but is so strongly affected by the performance of others that it tells us very little about the individual.

The case of the concert singer and the accompanist has been frequently described in musical memoirs. If the pianist plays the music exactly as it is written, he will spoil the singer's performance without making his own performance look very good. If he follows the singer as closely as possible, adapting to unscheduled changes of tempo and missed notes, the performance will go better but his own musicianship may appear deficient unless the singer is meticulous. If he has a grudge against the singer, the accompanist can destroy the latter's performance without any visible effort. Although the singer's performance is somewhat more dependent upon the accompanist than vice versa, the two of them are so closely entwined as to make it hazardous to appraise either one without taking the influence of the other into account.

* The approximate proportion of the variance in future performance that is accounted for by past performance can be estimated by squaring the coefficient of correlation. In this case $r^2 = (.60)^2 = .36$.

In highly dramatized activities like politics and war, it may be impossible to separate the performance of a candidate from that of his campaign manager, or of a commander from that of his chief of staff, even under the conditions of high visibility in which they operate. As we move down the line into the relative obscurity of an organization's lower depths, the accurate assignment of credit and blame becomes progressively more difficult, and whether the lieutenant or the sergeant deserves the credit for making an effective platoon may be a question not answerable this side of heaven.

3. *The masking of individual performance by intermediate supervisors.* This is another kind of masking that is equally significant. When an intermediate supervisor in an organization is required to report to higher authority on the performance of his subordinates—as is the case in nearly all organizations—he does not necessarily react in a straightforward way. From what he knows about the organization's habits, he may anticipate that if he reports an outstandingly good performance he may lose some of the credit he would otherwise get for himself, or risk losing the subordinate by promotion or transfer, or disrupt an effective team because of the jealousy aroused by the special recognition of one of its members. His motives for not reporting an outstandingly bad performance may be equally compelling. At best, he invites the suspicion of trying to evade responsibility. At worst, he incurs blame for the poor supervision that made the poor performance possible.

Moreover, both favorable and unfavorable reports diminish the authority of the intermediate supervisor to some extent by taking rewards and punishments out of his hands and by giving the subordinate a reputation the supervisor may later be powerless to change. A very secure, high-ranking supervisor may not be troubled by these concerns, but the ordinary unit commander, foreman, school principal, or chapter president would report very little about individuals to higher headquarters if he had his druthers. Recognizing this, most large bureaucratic organizations have installed formal rating systems whereby supervisors at all levels are required to evaluate the performance of their subordinates in writing at frequent intervals and to send their ratings upstairs. Which creates some new problems.

4. *The defects of rating systems.* Hundreds of ingenious rating

systems have been devised and put into effect in modern bureaucracies, but, with one significant exception we will mention
later, they can be reduced to a small number of categories: those
with or without a forced ranking of the persons rated, with or
without consultation between the rater and the person rated, with
or without the participation of the peers and subordinates of the
person rated. Each of these alternatives has its characteristic pitfalls, and a systematic review of them may lead you to feel that the
whole enterprise is haunted, which indeed it is.

When the rater is not required to compare the persons he rates
or to place them in a rank order, but is allowed to arrange them
against an absolute standard on a scale of, for example, outstanding, excellent, good, fair, and poor, there will be an almost
irresistible tendency for ratings to cluster at the high end of the
scale, with the great majority of those rated receiving at least "excellent," and nobody except the rater's sworn enemy receiving
"fair" or "poor." If the competitive pressure is very great, "outstanding" may become the normal grade. This occurs, for example,
in contests for government fellowships when professors rating the
work of their students suspect that anything less than "outstanding"
will disqualify the candidate in the first round. It also happens
whenever executives rate secretaries whom they want to keep.

The skewing of ratings toward the favorable end of the scale
is not overcome by requiring that fifteen or twenty traits be rated
separately. The experienced rater will throw in an occasional
"good" to break the monotonous string of "outstandings," but the
net effect is much the same. The only effective way to avoid skewing is to require the rater to put all the persons he rates in rank
order of excellence, or to adhere to a formula that limits the number of high ratings he may give. These methods take care of the
skewing problem at the price of making the rating system both
inaccurate and unjust, since the best member of the worst group is
then rated higher than the average member of the best group,
against all common sense. The overall result is to depress the ratings of all individuals in good groups, as well as to stimulate jealousy and bitterness among co-workers.

Some of this bitterness can be avoided if ratings of performance are kept secret from the persons rated, and this is still done
in many organizations, although less frequently than it once was.

One defect of a secret rating system is that it gives the person rated no opportunity for self-improvement. Another defect is that it allows a supervisor to carry out a secret vendetta against an unknowing subordinate and to stab him down without fear of reprisal. I knew of one such case in a famous research laboratory where a section director accomplished the dismissal of a promising young scientist by a series of strongly negative ratings in order, as it turned out later, to make a place for his ambitious mistress.

The practice now followed in most well-regulated bureaucracies is for the rater to sit down with the ratee and discuss the ratings. One or both of them may be required to certify in writing that the conversation actually took place. This prevents the secret vendetta but makes a candid appraisal difficult unless the rater is so powerful that he is in no way dependent on the ratee's goodwill, and provided that the rater is allowed to use an absolute standard and is not compelled to rank the ratee against close associates. The Greek legend of the judgment of Paris ("This golden apple is for the fairest") nicely illustrates what happens in any organization when the compulsory ranking of the persons rated is combined with the compulsory disclosure of the ratings. The judgment of Paris, you will remember, provoked the Trojan War.

Some organizations, challenged by these profundities, have worked out a schizoid rating system whereby raters, in effect, keep two sets of books. A rating against an absolute standard skewed in the usual way is discussed with each ratee and plans are laid for his improvement. Another rating placing all ratees in comparative rank order is secretly compared at the same time and sent upstairs to be used as a guide for assignments and promotions. Such organizations are wicked and deserve most of what happens to them.

There is an inherent bias in any supervisory rating in that supervisors are likely to give higher ratings to their more compliant subordinates, even in situations where submissiveness is not relevant to good performance. In his *Management and Machiavelli*, Antony Jay devotes two chapters to this problem. The gist of his argument is that potential leaders are likely to be arrogant, and stubborn subordinates and are often forced out of the organization that needs them because of their unwillingness to fit into a mold of conformity.

One way to avoid supervisory bias in a rating system is to invite additional ratings of performance from an individual's peers and subordinates in order to obtain a kind of holograph of his performance that can be inspected from any angle. This is obviously a sound idea, but it does not always work out in practice. In the first place, it is almost essential that ratings by peers be kept secret in order to preserve the solidarity of the peer group, and that ratings by subordinates be kept secret also, in order to protect the raters from reprisal. But if the ratings are kept secret, they are only available to supervisors, and since the whole point of the exercise is that the ratings of peers and subordinates often disagree with supervisory ratings, they are likely to be disregarded.

Is it futile, then, for an organization to attempt to evaluate the performance of its individual members? Not at all. What *is* futile is the attempt to paper over inadequate information about an individual's performance with a show of objectivity. Before we consider better ways of evaluating performance, let us examine the most common situation in which a deficit of information about individual performance develops.

5. *Invisible performances.* Any complex organizational program includes many activities not ordinarily visible from the top, and some activities not ordinarily visible to anybody except the people directly engaged. The normal tendency of the normal manager is to assume that these invisible performances are going well unless there is some reason to think otherwise, and even in that case the responsible manager, like the husband of an unfaithful wife, may be the last to know what everybody else knows: that the cashiers are stealing from the till, the watchmen sleeping on duty, the mechanics working on their own cars, the file clerks throwing away more papers than they file, and the purchasing agent taking bribes.

The very worst maxim for a manager to believe is that no news is good news. In an organization, no news about the performance of an individual or a unit is sometimes good news and sometimes very bad news. I once observed a remarkable incident in the headquarters of a large voluntary association when one of the paid staff left town, settled in a ski lodge in a distant state, and stayed there for several months without attracting the attention of his immediate supervisors, who noticed his absence from staff meetings but concluded that he was "out in the field" and did not investigate further.

To assume that things are going well in any given corner of the organization because you hear no complaints and are not called upon to take action is always imprudent and may occasionally be fatal. The discovery that you lack solid information about the performance of an activity for which you are ultimately responsible ought to set off a quiet investigation without delay.

THE COMMON SENSE OF EVALUATION

The problems sketched out above do not have a single elegant solution, but they can be overcome in a practically satisfactory way by any manager who is willing to take the necessary trouble and to recognize and respect the sociological framework of the situation in which A passes judgment on B on behalf of an organization.

At the risk of oversimplification, the common sense of evaluating individual performance may be summarized as follows:

1. *Treat any evaluation as a useful estimate with a considerable margin of error.* Recognize that evaluations of individual performance are necessarily inconsistent and necessarily subjective, depending upon what aspect of the performance is being evaluated, and when, and by whom.

2. *Refrain from evaluating with insufficient information.* This is a simple and sensible rule, but it is often broken. It is a little embarrassing to admit that one has no idea what a subordinate does or how well he does it, but it is stupid to form opinions without evidence and shameful to act on such opinions.

3. *Hoard information about anyone you may have to evaluate.* This means all sorts of information: memos, correspondence, interview notes, work samples, formal and informal evaluations by others, recommendations, complaints, achievement tests. Even the performance of the most anonymous clerk in a large office or of a machine operator in a mass-production plant can furnish the material for an extensive, detailed, and highly informative individual record, as demonstrated by the employee performance record devised by J. C. Flanigan and R. K. Burns, and illustrated on

pages 154–55.[6] Such a record is at the other extreme from the usual rating scale and provides an infinitely better basis for judgment.

Another advantage of the critical-incident method of evaluation is that it gives us a picture of the person evaluated in relation to the evaluator, and thus makes us vividly aware that every evaluation is the outcome of a two-sided or multisided relationship, so that no person ever appears exactly the same in different relationships.

4. *Never evaluate people you do not know.* This may seem self-evident, but in the mumbo jumbo of bureaucratic personnel practices it is often forgotten. The important implication for the indirect supervisor is that with respect to anyone in the organization whom he does not know, he must delegate the responsibility for evaluation to a responsible subordinate whose recommendations he is prepared to accept. If this undermines the manager's claim to omniscience, so much the better.

Rewards and punishments

The people who participate in organizations are rewarded in pay, prestige, and privileges, by which rewards their morale is largely determined. Voluntary associations that do not offer pay must satisfy their members with even larger increments of prestige or privilege.

Systems of organizational reward are extraordinarily complex and diversified. But the manager's fundamental problem in distributing rewards is the same whether he is setting wages or handing out medals. That problem, in short, is how to offer sufficient incentives to keep up the morale of the organization's most valuable members without thereby lowering the morale of everybody else. It confronts every manager faced with a request for a salary raise or a recommendation for promotion. The problem is compounded in most organizations by the need to balance the claims of seniority against the claims of merit and the need for parity with other organizations in the same field.

Seniority and merit are never completely compatible. An organization that does not respect the claims of seniority can expect

A Detailed Employee Performance Record

Work Habits and Attitudes

9 Productivity

4	3	2	1
5		2 2/2 Kept on going	1 2/6 Did job on time
6			

3	2	1

a. Failed to do assigned task; b. Took more time than necessary; c. Slowed down unnecessarily; d. Worked at uneven tempo; e. Interfered with production line progress; f. Stopped equipment unnecessarily.

(A.) Worked efficiently despite obstacles; B. Was outstanding in the performance of his job; (C.) Avoided an opportunity to slack off.

10 Dependability

4	3	2	1
5		2 2/11 Told foreman ~~~~~	2/10 Checked parts
6			

3	2	1

a. Left work without leave; b. Was late for work; c. Stopped before quitting time; d. Took excessive relief; e. Failed to report for overtime work; f. Loafed at or between jobs; g. Did personal work as job; h. Neglected assigned task.

(A.) Did extra work during idle period; (B.) Anticipated and notified foreman that he would be out of work.

11 Accepting Supervision and Organizational Procedures

	1	2	3	4
				5
				6

4	3	2	1
5		2/5 uncomple Table	1 2/2 Refused to try new method
6			

a. Refused criticism, advice; b. Opposed instructions; c. Ridiculed foreman; d. Objected to, avoided, refused job change; e. Neglected to change desk, equipment; f. Was careless with materials, equipment; g. Kept same dirty, unworkable; h. Violated safety procedure; i. Distracted co-worker from job; j. Objected to, disobeyed shop rules.

A. Displayed unusual cooperation; B. Accepted disliked job without complaint; C. Accepted job change without resistance; D. Performed careful checks; E. Careful work reduced scrap, equipment damage; F. Salvaged parts, equipment; G. Cleaned, checked equipment for repair; H. Reported unsafe condition.

9A. Produced job on time despite interference on new construction going on.

9C. Did not stop machine during minor distraction.

10A. Checked parts while machine was being repaired. Saved time.

10B. Notified foreman job would be completed in two hours.

11a. Refused to try new, better method.

11g. Work table too cluttered to do job.

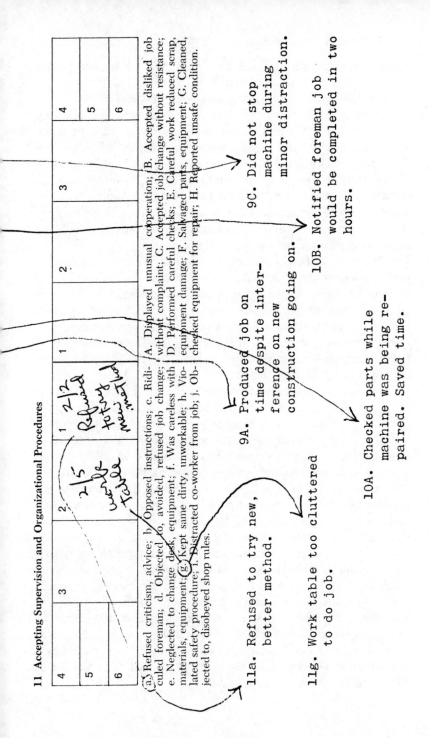

to have high turnover, which is bad for morale, while an organization that does not reward outstanding merit will lose its best people, which is bad for productivity and everything else.

In practice, most organizations of a given type lean one way or another. Railroads and government agencies reward seniority more than merit. Their morale tends to be moderately high and their productivity low. Athletic teams and advertising agencies reward merit without much regard to seniority. Their morale tends to fluctuate with competitive success. Some organizations follow a mixed policy. A naval officer is rewarded according to seniority in the early part of his career, and according to merit later on. The sequence is reversed for a university professor.

The organizations that can be relatively sure of maintaining high morale are those that offer an essentially equal reward to all of their members, such as exclusive clubs and honorary societies. In all other organizations, the maintenance of a high level of morale is a delicate and uncertain task, since productivity is maintained to a large extent by unequal rewards, which dissatisfy some members. It is the manager's responsibility to keep this dissatisfaction from turning into active resentment.

The distribution of punishments is as critical for morale as the distribution of rewards, and as delicate. Most modern organizations are diffident about punishment. Schools no longer flog, churches no longer excommunicate, workers are no longer fined for breaking factory rules. In some schools, nobody is ever kept back a grade, and in some minimum-security prisons, the only penalty for misconduct is to be transferred somewhere else. Nevertheless, every organization administers punishments in one way or another, and the subtle punishments of permissive organizations are sometimes sufficiently cruel. The school that prohibits any form of corporal punishment may encourage pupils to ostracize an uncooperative classmate. Where organizations formerly punished their recalcitrant members by direct deprivation, the modern organization relies mainly on relative deprivation. In other words, the individual is punished by not receiving a reward that others receive. Instead of having his pay lowered, he is excluded from an across-the-board raise. Instead of being demoted, he is passed over for a routine promotion, or his name is omitted from the list of those who receive a routine honor.

An unintended effect of the modern mode of punishment is that punishments are experienced where none are intended. In one instance I observed, the promotion of a woman in a group of accountants to the position of comptroller was experienced as a punishment by her female colleagues, who did not concede her superiority; by her male colleagues, who assumed they had a prior claim to promotion based on gender; by the old-timers in the office, who did not expect to get the job but felt that their experience had been devalued by the appointment of someone much less experienced; and perhaps most acutely by the comptroller's two secretaries, who experienced a complex loss of social and erotic status. Reactions of this kind are so common that, in some organizations, every promotion from within is a surefire disaster.

It stands to reason that you cannot expect people to be happy when they are passed over in favor of a close associate or when someone with similar experience and qualifications enjoys privileges from which they are barred. But as we noted at the beginning of this chapter, happiness is not the exact equivalent of morale, and, by the same token, unhappiness is not automatically converted into low morale. The catalyst is the sense of justice or injustice. Relative deprivation, when it is perceived as deliberately unjust, provokes disaffection with the organization. When it is not so perceived, the unhappiness soon passes and the effect on morale is only transitory.

For this reason, the primary concern of the manager in the administration of rewards and punishments must be to do justice, or rather, as Machiavelli pointed out long ago, to appear to do justice. But this qualification is not as Machiavellian as it seems. It merely reminds us that the manager's private conception of justice has no relevance to the morale of his subordinates. What matters is *their* conception of justice.

DISTRIBUTIVE JUSTICE

In recent years, the sociologists who specialize in the study of organizations have carried on a lively and interesting debate about the nature of distributive justice. According to one theory, the members of an organization perceive their treatment as just when the ratio of their efforts to their rewards is the same as the ratio of efforts to rewards obtained by other people around them, the effort, or "investment" being measured not only by the individual's sweat but by his seniority, skill, and responsibility.[7]

According to the opposing theory, the members of an organization perceive their rewards as just if and when their rewards are in line with their rank in the organization and their rank in the organization is in line with their qualifications.[8]

This theoretical controversy is not easily resolved by empirical evidence, although some ingenious laboratory experiments have tried to resolve it. For our present purposes, the points on which the two theories agree are more important than those on which they differ. Both theories say that the people who participate in organizational programs evaluate the rewards and punishments they receive in relation to the efforts they put forth, the sacrifices they make, their organizational status, and the rewards and punishments received by other people with whom they compare themselves in various ways. The essence of injustice is to receive less reward or more punishment than one expects on the basis of these comparisons. The key word is *expects*. "They did not treat me fairly" can generally be translated as "My rewards were less (or my punishments greater) than I expected from my knowledge of the organization's norms."

The sense of injustice springs spontaneously from any serious discrepancy between how the individual expects to be treated by the organization and how he is treated. When there is general agreement about what the norms are, the cry of injustice arises whenever the norms seem not to have been followed in a particular case or not to have been uniformly applied. During an organizational crisis, of course, the norms themselves may come under challenge and the organization may be accused of injustice because it follows a given norm when, considering its goals or its values, it might have been expected to follow another.

The members of an organization may receive very unequal rewards or punishments for nearly identical actions without provoking anyone's sense of injustice, provided that the inequality results from normal policy and procedure and is fully predictable. Indeed, it is probably impossible to discover any organization, no matter how small and simple, that treats its members so evenhandedly that the reward or punishment elicited by a given action is the same regardless of the actor. Most organizations have complex procedures—some explicit and some unconscious—for assuring appropriate inequality. These are never so simple as merely to give larger rewards and smaller punishments to persons of higher status, although their net effect may tend in that direction. For example, in almost every organization, a public expression of hostility to the organization by a high-ranking member elicits more punishment than the same expression by a low-ranking member.[9] The legendary "Man Without a Country," who was court-martialed and sentenced to lifetime confinement in exile for saying (under peculiar conditions), "I wish that I may never see or hear of the United States again," was necessarily an officer; the same comment by a common sailor would have led at most to a reprimand. On the other hand, the use of organizational facilities for private purposes by low-ranking members of an organization is likely to be severely punished, while the same conduct by someone of high rank would go unrebuked.

The individual's expectations are so critical in determining whether he perceives his treatment by the organization as just or unjust that a discrepancy in his favor may be nearly as demoralizing as one against him. Laboratory experiments show that when subjects in experimental work groups are led to believe they have been assigned a piecework rate of pay significantly higher than their qualifications entitle them to, their output drops sharply, and some subjects are so uncomfortable that they quit the experiment.

The ratio of treatment to expectation is so important in determining the individual's attitude toward an organization that it often blocks out the objective advantages or disadvantages of his situation. One of the minor discoveries made by Samuel Stouffer and his associates in their monumental study of the American army in World War II was that soldiers in units with frequent and easy promotions, such as air force squadrons, were consistently less satisfied with their promotion opportunities than equally qualified soldiers in units where promotions were rare and difficult, such as military police detachments.[10] The investigators' explanation, which seems to fit the facts, was that the frequent, easy promotions in the air force encouraged enlisted airmen to develop expectations that raced ahead of their actual opportunities, while the difficulty of promotion in the military police discouraged anyone from counting on it.

Nancy Scott's fascinating study of clerical workers under two styles of supervision found that an experimental group of clerks who were given considerable autonomy and allowed to work without close supervision had lower morale than a control group of clerks doing similar work under very close supervision. Interviews with the members of the experimental group disclosed that after they were given increased autonomy and responsibility they thought themselves entitled to higher pay than the clerks in the control group. They were so disgruntled at not receiving it that their output eventually declined to a much lower level than that of the control group.

Deleterious morale effects can be produced quite mechanically by procedures that foster rising expectations and then cut them off. In bureaucracies of the civil service type, skilled craftsmen, white-collar people, and technicians are customarily hired at the bottom of a salary range with provision for annual merit increases, until the top of the range is reached four or five years later. The cessation of the annual increase does not put a stop to the habit of anticipating an annual increase, with the result that many employees quit the organization within a year or two after reaching the top of their range. Similar effects may be observed among public school teachers and, with respect to intangible rewards, among social work volunteers. Indeed, any organization that encourages its rank-and-file participants, or some of them, to expect a continuously rising level of reward is certain to have severe morale problems sooner or later when the arithmetic of the situation puts a stop to further increments.

In most organizations, high-ranking members have much more to hope for than rank-and-file members. Their opportunities for promotion, remuneration, and honors are more numerous and involve much larger increments. It follows, by the same paradox we pointed out in the case of the airmen and military policemen, that they have more opportunities for disappointment, and that their disappointments are more severe. To just miss becoming executive vice-president is a greater blow than to just miss promotion to assistant janitor foreman. Thus, in most organizations, really severe morale problems commonly occur in the upper reaches of the hierarchy even though morale is generally correlated with status.

The disaffection of a high-ranking member of an organization often has calamitous consequences, as when a Benedict Arnold trades with the enemy for a promotion he was denied by his own side, or a Mr. Christian uses his authority as an officer to organize a successful mutiny.

Up to this point we have spoken about the treatment of individuals and their reactions, but groups, of course, also develop collective expectations and have them frustrated; and the excitement aroused in a group by such an event is amplified by social interaction so that, in many instances, the impact on morale is entirely disproportionate to the provocation. There is the typical situation in which a well-organized group suffers some small deprivation relative to another group but persuades itself, in the ensuing excitement, that its entire stake in the organization is menaced, and overreacts accordingly. Once aroused to a sense of having been unjustly treated, a group is not as easy to pacify as an individual, and when it has been pacified, its more intransigent members will probably continue to nurse their grudges for the next occasion.

All this adds up to a powerful incentive for any manager to avoid disappointing his subordinates in the distribution of rewards and punishments or, in other words, to deal justly with them in their eyes. The principles of organizational justice are as old as Hammurabi and fairly straightforward, but cannot always be followed in actual situations, inasmuch as it is not always possible to determine who will perceive himself as relatively deprived by a given action. I know of a candidate for public office who was gravely disaffected by the emphasis that the state organization of his party put on the campaign of a candidate in a neighboring district, even though he himself had participated in a decision to funnel more resources to the other candidate, who was running hard-pressed in a close race.

How to deal justly with subordinates   1. *Respect the equality of equals.* The most elementary violation of rough justice—as every schoolteacher, platoon sergeant, and precinct leader knows—is to give unequal treatment to persons or groups who are entitled to equal treatment in a given situation. The key words are *in a given situation.* In most organizations, hardly any pair of members can be found who are equal in every way, but it is difficult to find any pair of members who are not equal in some way. The children of a family, being unequal in age and sex, do not expect identical Christmas gifts from their parents, but they do expect gifts of approximately equal worth. The platoon noncoms have first choice of the available weapons but no more than an equal share of the available rations. The elected official has more political influence than the volunteer party workers, but the same single vote at the polls.

A manager ought never to create gratuitous inequalities between persons or groups who have a reasonable expectation of being treated equally in a given situation. Every manager does this some of the time—either inadvertently, because he fails to perceive that the assignment of duties or the allocation of resources in a particular way will disturb an existing relationship of equality, or intentionally, because he favors some people over their equals. In either case, the discrimination is always perceived as unjust and usually perceived as deliberate. The morale of the people who are disfavored invariably suffers, but the morale of those who are favored is not necessarily raised.

Providing equal treatment to equals often presents a logistical problem. What is to be done when there are not enough schoolbooks or rifles to go around, or when only one messenger can be sent on a mission of special opportunity? The best solutions to such problems are mechanical. Since no distribution of unequal treatment to parties who are entitled to equal treatment can be intrinsically just, the prudent manager refuses to be responsible for such a distribution and insists that the allocation be made by chance, as in drawing lots, or by rotation, or in some arbitrary order—alphabetically, by serial number, or by seniority, for example.

These last rubrics, if repeatedly used, turn into legitimate forms of inequality. In some schools, a pupil whose last name begins with *A* will sit in the front row of classrooms throughout his school career, while a pupil whose last name begins with Z will never leave the back row. In some egalitarian organizations, like certain monasteries, the entire treatment of an individual—his place in chapel and refectory, the work he does, and the privileges he enjoys within the house and outside—are mechanically regulated by seniority. So, in a very different world, are the assignments, routes, and work schedules of train crews on an American railroad.

2. *Respect legitimate inequality.* The equal treatment of persons or groups who are entitled to be treated unequally is resented —often with fury—by the disfavored party; to that extent it resembles the discriminatory treatment of equals, but there is an important difference. Whereas the favored party in the uneven treatment of equals often agrees with the disfavored party that the policy of favoritism is unfair, the favored party in the equal treatment of unequals seldom, if ever, agrees that any injustice has been done. *The natural tendency of distributive justice is toward equality of treatment.* If the ship's officers get berths with soft mattresses and the crew are given hard canvas cots, the crew may not perceive any injustice at all. The unequal treatment is conventional and contradicts no expectations. If the ship is remodeled and everybody gets the same comfortable berth, the officers will probably grumble, but it is inconceivable for the crew to agree that injustice has been done.[11]

In most organizations most of the time, there is some slack, so to speak, in the direction of equalization. The removal of some of the privileges of rank will not arouse very strong resistance on the part of those deprived, if their authority remains intact and the new arrangements do not interfere with their work. Municipal officials do not mutiny when their chauffeured limousines are taken away. But there is a line that a manager oversteps at his peril between equalizing the treatment of unequals and reversing the direction of inequality. Suppose that some of the ship's officers are asked to sleep on canvas cots after the crew has been given soft mattresses. They will not take it lying down. Or suppose that no parking spaces are provided for the private cars of the municipal officials who have just been deprived of their limousines. They will feel themselves driven to a choice between resigning and rebelling, and they will prefer to rebel if it is feasible. Either way, they will be moved to instantaneous hatred of the authority responsible for the decision.

3. *Prevent status incongruence.* Status incongruence is a condition in which interacting persons or groups in contact are unequal to each other in opposing directions within the same

organizational program: for example, when A supervises B, but B is better paid.

Status incongruence is deadly for morale. Both parties in such a relationship feel discriminated against, and, as a number of empirical studies have shown, they are likely to develop symptoms of emotional or bodily illness if the incongruence persists.

We do not have the space here to describe in detail the psychosocial mechanism that creates these effects, but its essential features are well known. Given two plausible but mutually exclusive characterizations of themselves, people normally tend to adopt the more favorable characterization and reject the other. But when an organization imposes incongruent statuses on its members, this choice becomes impossible for them. Their attempts to choose the more favorable characterization will be frustrated by the party or parties on the opposite end of the seesaw.

Incongruent status cannot be eliminated from an entire society. It is one of the standard causes of human misery. The distribution of skill is never congruent with the distribution of strength; the richest people are not the most intelligent; talent and virtue do not always go hand in hand, and when they do, they are not always rewarded. But within the limited jurisdiction of a single organization, most statuses can be kept congruent most of the time, and glaring cases of incongruence can be cured in one way or another.

Indeed, most of them can be prevented by fair-minded personnel policies, such as never withholding the perquisites and privileges that go with a particular position, never promoting a subordinate to a position of authority over his former superior, and recognizing demotion as well as promotion as a normal contingency in an organizational career.

Status incongruence is always less likely to develop if the organization provides its members with truthful information about their own prospects and is prepared to bear the costs of keeping it truthful.

4. *Keep promises.* This two-word sentence has all sorts of interesting corollaries. If every promise is to be kept, it follows that fewer promises should be made, and that is a good thing in itself. To promise rewards and not to provide them is a fundamental and flagrant type of injustice, as strongly resented in a nursery school as

in an executive suite. To promise punishment and then to withhold it is a good way of losing authority in any type of organization. The keeping of both sorts of promises is the first requisite of a just administration.

Most managers promise too much to too many people. Enthusiasm, fear, or an excess of optimism leads them to promise more than they can guarantee, for example, about the actions of their successors in office. I know an industrial executive with varied experience who says that he has never assumed a managerial position without being approached by subordinates to fulfill promises made by his predecessor.

It is fraudulent for a manager to promise more than he can deliver, and the problem is not relieved by putting the promise in contingent form—"if we have a profitable year," "assuming that the board approves." The promise will be remembered, while the contingency is forgotten or regarded as a formality.

Because promises are so important and memory so deceptive, the rare promises that are made by a manager should be in writing or, when that is not practicable, before reliable witnesses. Without this precaution, you will sooner or later have the experience of making some personal sacrifice in order to fulfill a promise to a subordinate and then be accused of bad faith.

By the same token, a promise should not be ambiguous. To make sure that it is not, its meaning must often be discussed at some length with all the parties involved.

The performance of a promise should be equally meticulous. To deliver a greater reward or a lesser punishment than has been promised is seldom advantageous. A promise made on behalf of an organization to one of its members represents a formal exchange between the organization and the member. The more literally the terms of exchange are followed, the more likely that both parties will be satisfied in the end. This principle extends beyond the narrow scope of managerial promises and can be applied to other transactions between the organization and its members.

5. *Observe due process.* Due process is a term borrowed from the courtroom, where it covers such matters as the right of a person accused of a crime to know the evidence against him, to confront his accuser, to summon witnesses on his behalf, to have legal counsel, to remain silent, to appeal an adverse decision, and many

related forms of protection that aim to establish an artificial parity between the excessively powerful state and the nearly helpless citizen during a criminal process, so that justice may be done.

Courtroom procedures are not appropriate for the working relationship between manager and subordinates, but the essential requirements of justice are much the same everywhere, and the procedures that insure fairness in well-governed organizations are analogous at many points to the formal requirements of due process. Let us state them as flatly as possible.

No accusation or claim against an individual in an organization should ever be acted upon without hearing his side of the story, allowing him to examine the evidence against him, and assisting him to obtain evidence on his own behalf.

Confrontation with an accuser is an uneasy business in a hierarchy, especially when the accuser is dependent upon the goodwill of the accused in one way or another and cannot be protected against reprisal. But there are obvious dangers, and a whiff of tyranny, in the practice of accepting anonymous accusations or complaints. On balance, I am inclined to think that the identity of an accuser must be revealed when his testimony is part of the evidence, but may be concealed from the accused if the accuser has done no more than call attention to existing evidence without adding any information to it.

We will probably want to go beyond courtroom procedure in one respect by destroying all record of an accusation or complaint that is judged, after investigation, to be malicious or mistaken.

The appearance of professional lawyers in an internal organizational transaction is generally a signal that the procedures of the organization have broken down or are about to do so. But every person accused or complained about ought to be able to obtain useful advice and to have a friend speak for him or appear for him at a hearing. In other words, due process implies a kind of inherent right to counsel.

An organization must respect its own rules and regulations when dealing with an individual. Its representatives may not reward or punish, convict or exonerate him without following a sequence of appropriate procedures: examining the evidence in a relevant way, obtaining and weighing the advice of people who are entitled to be consulted, and applying its own norms without deceit in the settlement of controversial matters. This means, among other things, that a manager ought not to connive at, or wink at, arbitrary actions by his subordinates that he would not permit to himself.

An essential element in due process is that persons in authority must take precautions to prevent themselves from following their own biases. The manager who wants to be just must delegate the right of judgment to others whenever his impartiality is subject to question. This implies, among other things, that he cannot judge a complaint directed against himself, that he ought not to hear a formal accusation against someone he loves or someone he detests, that he should call in others to evaluate the performance of anyone with whom he is closely connected, and that, where possible, he ought to provide channels of appeal for individuals on his own decisions concerning them. Such measures are often regarded as threatening by unsophisticated managers, but in practice they are much more likely to strengthen than to weaken managerial authority, reversing bad decisions and reinforcing good ones.

A serious commitment to due process will save an organization from the worst of those morale-shattering incidents that grow out of the maltreatment or alleged maltreatment of an individual and develop into raging conflicts between his supporters and his enemies. But due process, by itself, is no remedy for other types of factional conflict that are equally threatening to morale, to which we now turn our attention.

The containment of damaging conflicts

Outbreaks of hostility between individuals or groups can damage an organization by lowering its morale or its productivity, or both, and by driving people out of its program. Aside from the harm an uncontrolled conflict does to an organization, it is personally threatening to the manager; his inability to control it may lead to his overthrow, either by the angry contestants or by impatient bystanders.

Conflict, of course, is a basic social process; there is no conceivable way of removing all the conflict from an organization. Indeed, the existence of cooperation *within* groups implies some degree of conflict *between* groups, while ordinary social interaction is sustained by a mixture of friendly and hostile sentiments. Most of the conflicts that take place in an organization do not threaten its ongoing program and are not very painful to the people involved.

In general terms, conflict may be defined as social interaction between individuals or groups with incompatible goals. Some sociologists distinguish among *episodic conflicts,* which are intentionally staged according to rules accepted by all parties and give pleasure to participants and spectators; *continuous conflicts,* which are unplanned struggles between parties in a stable social system who have incompatible claims on that system; and *terminal conflicts,* in which the object of the parties is to destroy each other. Episodic conflicts present few problems for an organization. Continuous conflicts present many problems but cannot easily be prevented. The normal managerial goal is to prevent the development of terminal conflicts within the organization.

Terminal conflicts in organizations need not involve bloodshed, although they arouse bloodthirsty emotions. In a terminal conflict between individuals, the object of at least one of the parties is to remove the other from their common field of action or to render him helpless in it. A terminal conflict between groups involves similar motives, with the additional possibility that one group may seek to annex the other.

Once ignited, a terminal conflict is always costly. At best, the normal pattern of cooperation is disrupted for a period of time; at worse, the organization will sustain a massive loss of resources and personnel, and may break up entirely. When a definitive victory is scored in terminal conflict, the losing side is likely to desert the organization. When there is a stalemate, both parties may be forced out. The full effects may be felt only in the long run, but even in the short run, any terminal conflict in an organization is likely to induce a deterioration of morale that spreads far beyond the immediate participants.

The manager who attempts to settle one of these little wars after it has gotten well started will find himself caught in the curious trap that Herbert A. Shepard observed in the management laboratory at Ann Arbor, Michigan, when two face-to-face groups of about a dozen members were given the same problem to solve competitively and a judge was appointed to listen to both solutions and name a winner. "Individuals may be good losers, but groups almost never are," the investigator remarked. The judge received no credit or thanks from either side in these contests. The winning group invariably thought it had the better solution and therefore owed the judge no thanks for the favorable decision, while the losing group attributed the same decision to bias or stupidity.[12]

The same fatal mechanism may work against the manager who attempts to arbitrate a conflict between two strong subordinates, with the additional embellishment that *both* parties may find his decision unacceptable and turn their combined fury against him.

A manager with the wisdom of Solomon may occasionally be able to suggest a settlement that is fully acceptable to both of the parties locked in a death struggle, but the odds against doing it often are overwhelming. It is infinitely easier to prevent conflicts from escalating into the terminal phase than to settle them after they have escalated. The better practice is to concentrate on nipping them in the bud, and when that fails, to work on isolating the trouble as quickly as possible.

FOUR TYPES OF CONFLICT AND WHAT TO DO ABOUT THEM

The scenarios of organizational conflict are many and varied, but every manager has to deal sooner or later with four stock situations: (1) a personal feud between two key members of the organization; (2) the alleged persecution of a subordinate by a superior; (3) the breakdown of cooperation between two related departments; (4) a schism between ideological factions.

Each of these stock situations has certain standard features that make it possible for us to talk about what a manager can do to prevent or contain such disturbances without limiting the discussion to particular cases.

The development of a *personal feud* between two key members of an organization is typically marked by an accumulation of mutual grievances: the interruption, at first, of sociable communication and, later, of all communication; a growing paranoia, as each of them discovers the actions of the other by hearsay and interprets them with suspicion; and a progressive recruitment of

friends and associates to join the hostilities. The disturbance of
normal working relationships eventually extends far beyond the
broken relationship between the principal parties, so that the
manager who succeeds in remaining neutral may be distrusted and
eventually hated by both sides.

The best strategy for resolving a personal feud between two
key members of your organization is remarkably simple: *take one
side or the other.*

This advice may seem surprising, but a little reflection will
show good reasons for it. We are dealing, remember, with an
emotional crisis, not a rational argument that can be resolved by
discussion. Many feuds do begin with rational arguments, but as
the emotional crisis develops, the original issues are left far behind.
Some feuds are not based on organizational issues at all. The most
bitter feud I have ever observed in an organization began when
one vice-president had a weekend affair with another's married
secretary.

Once kindled, a feud between persons of approximately equal
organizational power is not likely to be extinguished. Assuming
that both persons are valuable to the organization, the manager
who intervenes has a double purpose: to prevent them from drawing in other people, and to keep them both in the organization, if
possible.

By giving full support to one of the feudists, preferably the
stronger, the manager furthers both these purposes. First, the conflict becomes much less inviting to bystanders because the reinforced party no longer needs help and the other party's cause is
much less promising. Second, the danger that both people may
quit in anger is effectively averted. The one supported by the
manager has no motive to quit. The loser may walk out, of course,
but he is somewhat less likely to do so than if the feud had been
allowed to run its full course. It may be easier for him to make
peace in the face of overwhelming odds than it would have been in
a more equal struggle.

The *alleged persecution of a subordinate by a superior* needs
to be handled differently, since the problem it poses for the organization is quite different. Whereas a feud out of control may split
the organization down the middle, a grievance out of control may
spark off a rebellion that splits it horizontally. Moreover, in this

situation the manager is not much concerned about losing people. The alleged persecutor will not experience much pressure to quit unless matters get completely out of hand, and whether the alleged victim goes or stays is relatively unimportant, from the organization's standpoint.

The manager who wants to intervene in an incident of this kind has very limited options. If he supports the alleged persecutor, who already has a preponderance of power, he creates the impression of being indifferent to justice. If he supports the alleged victim, he breaks the bond of loyalty between himself and his subordinate and runs the risk of alienating other subordinates who feel threatened by the incident.

The best method of handling an alleged persecution was suggested in the second chapter in connection with grievance procedures: *delegate responsibility for investigating and settling the complaint to an impartial agent.*

This procedure has several related advantages. It protects the manager from taking action on a biased view of the facts, which he is otherwise likely to do because his communications with the higher-ranking party to the conflict are so much better. It protects the complainant from reprisals by his superior. It introduces a wholesome delay that interrupts the accumulation of tension. And most important, it demonstrates that the organization is committed to evenhanded justice, which, as noted before, is the real foundation of morale.

The *breakdown of cooperation between related departments* of an organization normally occurs in connection with a boundary dispute. If we examine in detail the development of such a dispute, we almost always discover that one department is perceived by another as encroaching upon its territory or functions and that the refusal of routine cooperation is either a device for checking the alleged encroachment or a protest against it.

Such situations have to be investigated carefully before any positive action can be taken. It sometimes turns out that a boundary dispute can be settled out of hand either because it arose from a simple misunderstanding or because one of the parties is plainly in the wrong. More often, it will be found that both departments have a reasonable claim to the disputed territory or function, and in that case it is most unlikely that the quarrel can be settled by bringing the parties together and letting them talk it out.

About the only way to put a stop to a boundary dispute is to *reorganize the departments or the disputed territory or function so that the boundary is unmistakable.*

As a participant-observer in a New England factory some years ago, Orvis Collins noted that all of the executives were Yankees and all the foremen were Irish. When a central janitor service was organized under the auspices of the labor-management committee, a deadlock arose over the question of who should be in charge of the janitor service. The labor members of the committee, visualizing the post as janitor-foreman, insisted on an Irish candidate. The management members, who regarded the position as an executive one, refused to accept the Irish nominee. The problem was resolved when top management ordered the position classified as "sanitation engineer" and then, as a matter of course, appointed a Yankee.[13]

Such a proceeding may seem high-handed, but it causes much less trouble than an attempt to mediate a boundary dispute without reorganization. Most boundary disputes occur in the first place because of managerial confusion or indecisiveness.

The most difficult kind of conflict to resolve in an organization is a *schism between ideological factions* over a point of principle. One faction in the church wants to retain the traditional liturgy; the opposing faction wants the liturgy modernized. One faction in a civic association wants to stay out of politics; the other faction believes that the association's goals can be achieved only through politics. One faction in the union preaches long-term cooperation with employers; the other faction wants to give them hell. And so on. Nearly every live organization contains the germs of one or more of these ideological divisions, but they turn into full-blown schisms only under certain conditions, to wit: one or more ambitious and devoted leaders in each faction; an outraged reaction to some particular incident that provokes the mobilization of one faction and countermobilization by the other; the imminence of major decisions that seem to involve a choice between the opposing ideologies.

The manager of an organization split by schism cannot remain above the battle because he cannot seem to ignore any ideological issue taken so seriously by other members. But he cannot support either faction without jeopardizing his claim to be the leader of the whole organization. The only way out of this dilemma is to seek and find a genuine compromise between the two factions, based on a synthesis of their opposing positions. Any other policy risks the organization's future, if only because ideological disputes arouse passions all out of proportion to the practical interests involved. "The reason why controversies of this kind are so terribly bitter," said Dean Courtney Brown in the course of an argument about educational ideology, "is that the stakes are so *low*." And indeed, there is some reason to believe that the less the protagonists have at stake, the more bitter an ideological schism may become, since there is little pressure to reach a compromise when there are no practical interests to be protected.

The strategy for resolving a schism in an organization may be stated thus: *bring the factions together, force them to work out a mutually acceptable compromise, and then throw all your weight behind the compromise.*

This procedure is not foolproof or trouble-free, but it is clearly the best procedure to follow. The fools most likely to cause trouble are the zealots of either faction. The typical troubles are that it takes a great deal of time, work, and emotional wear and tear to find an acceptable compromise, and that, in the course of protracted negotiations, the representatives of each faction are likely to lose touch with the people they represent, who have not undergone the instructive experience of being forced to descend from their fighting platforms and grapple with complex issues. I once sat with an eighteen-member committee appointed to work out a compromise between two bitter factions in a large public institution, the one favoring continued growth and the other demanding a policy of stabilization. Most of the members of the committee, when originally appointed, were fanatical partisans of one side or the other, and the meetings, under the chairmanship of the institution's second-in-command, began in an atmosphere of deep mistrust. But after seven months of meeting two or three times a week, often far into the night, and of examining thousands of pages of evidence and hearing scores of witnesses, the committee found that a detailed compromise pretty nearly wrote itself and commanded the nearly unanimous support of the committee. Things did not go quite as smoothly when the committee members reported back to their respective factions; some of them were roughly treated. Each faction developed a minority of diehards who rejected the compromise and those associated with it. But in the long run, and with strong support from the institution's chief executive, the compromise proved irresistible.

This brief treatment does not exhaust the possibilities of internal conflict within an organization, but it does cover those that pose a major threat to morale, and the manager who can successfully contain the four types of eruption just described has reason to feel confident about the organization's morale.

How to recognize high morale

The indicators of a high level of morale vary somewhat from one organization to another and are occasionally deceptive, but a manager can be reasonably satisfied if he observes that:

1. In the course of his organizational activities, he never encounters small clusters of people who scatter furtively at his approach.

2. Although lateness and absenteeism occur, they never seem to interfere with the organizational program.

3. The turnover rate is stable or declining. Few people leave voluntarily except for compelling personal reasons.

4. The people who are recruited to fill vacant positions generally seem to be better qualified than the people they replace.

5. Recruits are absorbed very quickly into the informal social network.

6. Everyone in the organization seems to know what his job is, and agreement about the organization's purposes is taken for granted.

7. Decisions to hire, fire, promote, or demote are usually unanimous, or nearly so, among those consulted.

8. Dismissals and demotions are rare and do not require elaborate precautions.

9. Ratings are not taken very seriously, but those in a supervisory position know a great deal about the people who report to

them and are willing to pass such information on to their superiors.

10. There is relatively little discussion of pay and privileges, since the existing distribution is taken for granted most of the time.

11. Organizational ceremonies are always well attended.

12. The manager is seldom called upon by subordinates to help maintain their authority.

13. People who get involved in organizational conflicts are apologetic about it, not complacent. And they do not stop greeting each other.

14. The manager's intervention in a conflict is usually welcomed by both sides.

5:Change

> *Suppose that a football reformer observed*
> *the obvious fact that the object of the game is*
> *to make touchdowns. This would lead immediately*
> *to the important discovery that if the two teams*
> *would only cooperate, hundreds of*
> *touchdowns could be made in a game,*
> *while only one or two of them are made when*
> *each opposes the other.*
>
> THURMAN ARNOLD

Change and innovation

No organization exists in a vacuum. Every organization must submit to the demands of its environment, and these demands vary as the environment changes. Even the most passive organization is compelled to modify itself from time to time in response to irresistible changes in its environment. A well-known study of a civic association was published under the title, "The Reluctant Organization and the Aggressive Environment," and the title tells the whole story. The organization in question sought to do as little as possible, but other civic associations pushed and pulled it into one new activity after another.

On the other hand, impulses toward change often appear in an organization without any outside stimulus. Organizations, like individuals, engage in campaigns of self-improvement. Many large organizations have planning departments to insure a constant

176

stream of innovations. Planning, however, does not protect an organization from unforeseen changes: in the first place, it cannot control the external environment, and in the second place, carefully planned changes in one part of an organization usually cause unexpected stresses in other parts.

The most elementary forms of organizational change are growth and decline. Few human organizations come to rest at the exact equilibrium point between growth and expansion. Most organizations, at any given time, are either expanding or contracting. Within limits, both processes are cumulative. Growth facilitates further growth; decline paves the way for further decline. Turning points are relatively infrequent. An organization may grow continuously from the time it is founded until it reaches a turning point and then decline continuously until it disappears.

Growth and decline call for numerous adjustments in an organization, and that is where we begin our discussion of the manager's responsibility for adaptation to change. Thereafter, we will consider the other types of adaptation required by market pressures, social change, technological change, creative innovation, and systematic planning.

Growing, stable, and declining organizations

In many fields of activity, such as banking and politics, an organization's growth rate is a direct measure of success. The growing organization has certain natural advantages. Its expanding resources pay for past mistakes and offer protection against current risks. The expansion of its program creates new opportunities for people in the organization and makes it easier to attract desirable recruits. Decision-making is relatively easy, or seems easy, because good decisions are confirmed, and poor decisions are masked, by continuing growth. The decision-maker has a wider range of choices than he would have in a stable or declining organization.

For the very same reasons, it is easy to make mistakes in the management of a growing organization, even if the mistakes do not show. It is probably harder to run a growing organization really well than to run the same type of organization in a stable phase. And the more rapid the growth, the more difficult the assignment.

MANAGERIAL PROBLEMS IN GROWING ORGANIZATIONS

It stands to reason that a manager of given energy and skill can control a smaller organization more firmly than a larger one, supervise more of its activity directly, observe more of what goes on, and understand a larger proportion of the relationships his subordinates have with each other and with outsiders. As the organization grows, control becomes more difficult by the simple accretion of numbers. There are ways of minimizing the damage by delegating responsibility and installing better data systems, but there is no way of avoiding it altogether.

The diminution of consensus about organizational values and goals is a normal consequence of growth, attributable in part to the inherent difficulty of getting a larger number of people who know each other less well to agree about anything, in part to the importation of new people and ideas, but mostly to the brute fact that as an organization grows, its relationships to its members and to the environment necessarily change, so that its original values and goals become somewhat incongruent with its current program. These problems are magnified by discontinuities of scale. An organization cannot grow indefinitely in small increments. Sooner or later it makes a quantum leap that transforms its whole character: the company acquires a second factory in another state; the family has its first child; a summer camp adds a winter program. Often the people involved do not realize that anything significant has occurred until they discover by hard experience that their familiar procedures no longer work and that their familiar routines have been bizarrely transformed.

One sign of discontinuity is the breakdown of organizational norms. There is a point in the growth of nearly every organization when internal theft becomes a problem and new security measures must be devised. In growing organizations that are badly run, a kind of criminal underground may develop.

The growth of an organization makes some of its people obsolete. As the organization grows, some of its original members—perhaps those who deserve most of the credit for its growth—will be unwilling or unable to adjust to the new order that growth produces, and will be abandoned by the wayside.

While the growing organization discards some of its insiders, its dependence on outsiders increases, because the expanded program requires transactions with an expanded environment or because growth has been achieved by mortgaging resources or assuming other long-term commitments. Most successful private enterprises in the United States have gone this route, sacrificing independence for growth and ending up either under the control of outside investors or as subsidiaries of larger companies.

The problems of managing a growing organization are not insurmountable, but they do become more severe as the rate of growth accelerates, and organizations that grow very rapidly are often managed so badly that they ultimately collapse, as happened to so many of the corporate conglomerates formed in the United States in the 1960s.

The standard methods for coping with rapid expansion in an organization (of any size) are:

1. team management
2. the decentralization of operating responsibilities
3. the standardization of procedures
4. the centralization of financial control
5. an expansion of communication facilities.

This formula, although derived from case studies of organizations of varying size, bears a close resemblance to the Sloan plan for General Motors that we discussed in the third chapter. The resemblance is not coincidental, since the Sloan plan was, in fact, designed for a rapidly expanding organization and worked well for upward of forty years until General Motors reached a level of relative stability and began to encounter a different set of problems. The same organization that had coped so well with the problems of expansion became remarkably clumsy and maladroit when asked to cope with such problems as the consumer attack led by Ralph Nader, the government's insistence on safety equipment and pollution controls, and the design constraints introduced by the energy crisis of the 1970s.

Although the formula set forth above calls to mind a giant

organization, I have seen it applied with notable success to middle-sized and even tiny organizations—a piano company expanding into the manufacture of electric organs, a civic orchestra in the process of becoming a full-time professional orchestra, a research institute outgrowing the converted barn in which it started.

Under team management, the single, ultimately responsible head of the organization to whom this book is addressed sometimes becomes two or three people who divide the job up or do it jointly.[1] More commonly under team management; the head of the organization can still be identified but has one or two close associates whose authority is nearly equal to his own. The reason for team management in rapidly expanding organizations is that there are at least three separate managerial jobs to be done: running the existing operation, supervising the expansion, and coping with the unpredictable problems that expansion creates.

But since there are built-in limits to the size of a managerial team (no executive committee is likely to function well with more than five members), the continued expansion of an organization continuously threatens to overload the management team unless the responsibility for routine and subsidiary operations is spun off as soon as possible to subordinate managers. Hence the need for decentralization. Decentralization is only feasible, however, if procedures are standardized and financial controls are tightened; otherwise it leads to anarchy. There remains the danger that the organization's ability to react to events as a unit will suffer because ts decentralized parts lack a common viewpoint. Hence the need ror expanded communications.

MANAGERIAL PROBLEMS IN STABLE ORGANIZATIONS

By a stable organization, I mean one that is not growing or declining significantly. It need not be stable in all other respects.

Some organizations are inherently stable because they are designed to operate with a membership of fixed size—a troupe of aerialists, for example, or a string quartet, or a state legislature. Some, such as the Central Mental Hospital described by Erving Goffman in his notable book on asylums,[2] must adapt their rosters and their activities to a given set of buildings and facilities, and therefore they have an approximately fixed size.

Some other organizations are stable by deliberate choice, steering a careful course between the temptation to grow and the danger of declining. A considerable number of small communities and small associations are run this way, and even a few sizable businesses. One Great Lakes shipping line, for example, operated the same fleet of eleven bulk carriers out of the same port for a period of thirty-two years, spanning the entire career of one fleet manager, without adding or losing a single ship and without ever replacing a captain for any reason but retirement.

As a general rule, morale is higher in stable organizations than in either growing or declining ones, but that is not to say that the stable organization is free of problems. There is the constant problem of assuring that the measures taken to prevent growth do not overcarry and lead into a spiral of decline. Stable organizations tend to be inflexible and set in their ways, and since they generally have low turnover they are apt to become more inflexible as their members age. The ragged, long-bearded crew of the Flying Dutchman's ship, as described in the old sea legend, were not unlike the personnel of some other organizations that have been stable for a long time. A middle-aged colleague of mine who joined the staff of a famous and extremely stable scientific institute in Paris said that he felt conspicuous at staff meetings because he was the only person present with no cane or hearing aid.

Because of their built-in resistance to change, stable organizations are inherently vulnerable to certain types of crisis. Crises of succession, when they occur in stable organizations, are especially severe, partly because the frustration of expectations in a stable organization is a more serious matter than in a dynamic organization, and poor decisions are almost irrevocable. I knew a man who served for seventeen years as the associate director of a stable industrial laboratory, secure in the knowledge that when the director reached the mandatory retirement age, the place would be his, and that he would then have fourteen more years to run the laboratory before his own retirement. In due course, the director retired and, to everybody's surprise, a younger man from outside was selected for the post. My friend's reactions were violent, running from initial disbelief to a near state of shock and finally into a nearly suicidal depression that required him to take a long leave of absence. When he recovered, he returned to work in his old job, but with a quiet hatred of the organization and the fixed intention of taking revenge at the first opportunity. As it turned out, the new director was sufficiently incompetent to fail in his job even without my friend's assistance. Between them, they wrecked the laboratory beyond repair within two years.

Such disasters are avoidable, however, provided that the stable organization refrains from actions—such as disrupting an orderly succession—that are incompatible with long-term stability. Some Oxford and Cambridge colleges have remained stable for centuries. The best account of how such an organization handles a crisis of succession may be found, lightly disguised as fiction, in C. P. Snow's novel *The Masters*, in which the fellows of a Cambridge college, selecting their new head in a bitterly contested election, take elaborate account of the motives and expectations of all concerned in order to arrive at the least disruptive choice.

The principal elements of a formula for managing a stable organization are these:

1. Adherence to traditional procedures
2. Slow-moving, intensive problem-solving efforts
3. Democratic participation in decision-making
4. Meticulous and easily accessible records and accounts
5. A system for the designation of successors primarily designed to prevent surprises.

A stable organization cannot be maintained for long unless it has the wholehearted support of its members and they maintain a vigilant lookout for any signs of incipient growth or decline. In order for the organization to obtain that much support from its members, it must contrive that their expectations will rarely be disappointed, and in order to do that, it must necessarily follow a conservative, thoughtful, and participatory mode of problem-solving. The manager of a stable organization is less of an initiator and more of a representative than the managers of growing and declining organizations, and his success is measured by how well he understands and expresses the wishes of his constituents.

MANAGERIAL PROBLEMS IN DECLINING
ORGANIZATIONS

Organizations decline for a variety of reasons, not all of which signify failure. A few types of organization have a built-in, normal rate of decline. An organized alumnae group, like the Old Ivy class of 1975, begins its existence with a maximum roster and declines over the years as members die or are lost from sight, until it is extinguished sixty or seventy years later. Veterans' organizations follow a similar course. Some very important types of organization anticipate cyclical decline as a matter of course. Standing armies and navies grow rapidly in wartime and decline even faster when a war comes to an end. Some organizations are plunged into a decline by achieving their original goals. The organizations formed to combat tuberculosis and poliomyelitis are classic, much-studied examples.

Tax-supported agencies decline if their appropriations are reduced. Schools, hospitals, and other service institutions decline when shifts of population reduce the demand for their services. A commercial enterprise may decline because of shrinking markets. The producers of washtubs, laundry soap, bluing, and other materials for hand laundry have been selling their products in a shrinking market for many years since the invention of washing machines.

As a general rule, it is much more difficult to manage a declining organization than a stable or growing one. The growing organization is rarely confronted by a truly insoluble problem—there is usually some way around it. The stable organization has learned to keep insoluble problems at bay, or it would not be stable. The declining organization, by contrast, is likely to have multiple problems that cannot be solved by any conceivable effort of its own.

Morale is usually low in declining organizations. Because of the organization's diminishing ability to meet its commitments, it must often disappoint the legitimate expectations of its members. In addition, they experience a kind of automatic status deflation as the organization's importance diminishes and the importance of their own activities is correspondingly reduced. When the decline of an organization is unscheduled, there is bound to be a loss of confidence in its procedures and in its goals, and this is likely to occur even when the decline is scheduled. Few professional groups are less certain of their own purposes than the officers of a peacetime army. This loss of confidence breeds cynicism and encourages corruption. Declining organizations are susceptible to abuse, exploitation, and looting by their own members.

The productivity of declining organizations is typically low because of inadequate resources to keep up with technological progress and the difficulty of recruiting and holding competent personnel.

A specific malady that afflicts declining organizations may be called "Parkinsonitis," after the brilliant satirist who invented Parkinson's Law.[3] Its leading symptom is the expansion of administrative overhead as the operations of a declining organization contract. This should not be confused with the tendency for administrative contraction to lag behind the contraction of other functions, which is almost inevitable in a declining organization. In a case of Parkinsonitis, the number of administrators and the costs of administration actually increase with each decrease in the number of people and activities to be administered. Parkinson presented figures for the Royal Navy between 1914 and 1928. During that period, the number of capital ships in commission decreased by 68 percent and the number of naval personnel by 32 percent, while the number of Admiralty officials increased by 78 percent, from 2,000 to 3,569. Another set of figures presented in the same essay showed a nearly fourfold increase in the staff of the British Colonial Office between 1935 and 1954, the period during which the colonial empire administered by that office was being liquidated.

The new manager of a declining organization starts with two strikes against him. First, he is sure to encounter innumerable frustrations. Second, his chances of ultimate success are poor. Nevertheless, even declining organizations need to be managed, and there is the consoling thought that failure in the management of a declining organization is not much of a disgrace, while success is a notable achievement.

The formula for managing a declining organization might be summarized as follows:

1. Reduce administrative overhead at a faster rate than the shrinkage of other activities.

2. Distinguish by careful analysis the essential and nonessential parts of the organizational process.

3. Eliminate as rapidly as possible the nonessential parts of the organizational program, and reinvest the resources saved in the essential parts.

4. Identify the persons or departments who are most conspicuously inefficient or corrupt and remove or reorganize them one by one.

5. Develop a new structure for communication and consultation, and use it to mobilize an inner circle of reformers in support of necessary reorganizations.

6. When the organization has been stripped of its nonessential functions and purged of its worst abuses, look for new activities and goals that may reverse the organization's decline.

Adjusting to market pressures

Aside from the permanent decline that leads to extinction, every healthy organization is susceptible to temporary phases of decline due to the market pressures caused by competition, scarcities, rising costs, or declining revenue.

COMPETITION

Every organization in the world competes with other organizations for resources, influence, manpower, and clients. Most organizations are simultaneously involved with several separate and distinct sets of competitors. A manufacturer of table linen competes, of course, with other linen manufacturers but also with importers, with manufacturers of paper napkins, plastic tablecloths, place mats, and disposable fabrics, and with commercial linen services and discount houses that buy linen from captive suppliers.

A noncommercial organization has similarly diversified competitors. A private liberal arts college, for example, competes intensely and consciously with other colleges in its league—in the same region, similarly organized, and of comparable prestige. But it is also involved willy-nilly in competition with a wide range of publicly supported institutions from state universities down to community colleges, and with a variety of alternative institutions such as vocational schools, service academies, and programs of educational travel.

When market conditions are highly favorable, as they were in the 1960s for the manufacturers of table linen and for liberal arts colleges, competitive efforts are directed almost exclusively against organizations in one's local set—against the other middle-size manufacturers of fine table linen, or against the other second-rank New England women's colleges. When market conditions turn unfavorable, the competitive focus shifts to more remote but more threatening competitors: the paper goods industry, the community colleges. The most successful competitors are generally those able to see the change of competitive focus coming a little ahead of their peers.

SCARCITIES

The most dangerous kind of market pressure is an absolute scarcity of something the organization requires for its program. A relative scarcity of material or manpower will be reflected, of course, in rising costs, and a relative scarcity of clients and customers will take the form of declining revenues. An absolute scarcity is a different sort of problem, and not particularly uncommon.

An absolute scarcity occurs when, for example, a source of supply or demand is cut off: the balsa wood used for model planes is no longer available because of a trade embargo; no doctors can be hired for the county hospital because physicians' services have been priced out of reach of rural hospitals; the Sunday school must be abandoned because the congregation has aged and has few young children; the municipal auditorium is condemned after a fire and there is no other hall large enough for the civic orchestra's concerts; a government ban on burning soft coal shuts off the fuel supply of the foundry that makes ornamental cast iron; the abandonment of air service to an island resort keeps all the tourists away; the exhaustion of the silver lode closes down the mine and the mining town.

An absolute scarcity cannot be argued with or fiddled with. It calls for bold, imaginative, and *quick* innovation, before the organization founders.

RISING COSTS

Rising costs may reflect the appearances of relative scarcities, as when a poor flax crop raises the price of linen or a shortage of psychological counselors increases the salaries that must be offered to hire one. But there are many other reasons why costs rise, some of them internal to the organization, such as ineffective administration, worn-out equipment, or embezzlement; some of them external, such as new taxes, increased postal rates, or general inflation. Some of these factors raise costs gradually, but others work abruptly so that, for example, every rise in fourth-class postage rates spells the end for some magazines, and every extension of minimum-wage coverage puts a stop to various small enterprises. The effect of rising costs is most dramatic when the organization is not free to pass on increases to its customers or clients. But even when it is, there comes a point where further increases reduce total revenues. That is the problem that faces private liberal arts colleges. Their tuition fees are already very high in relation to the ability of students' families to pay, and further increases to meet rising costs drive so many students away to publicly supported institutions that total revenues decline. Urban mass-transit systems have been caught in a similar spiral for many years. Increasing costs of labor, fuel, and equipment force them to increase their fares periodically, but every increase reduces the number of passengers, which soon calls for a further increase of fares, which reduces the number of passengers still more, and so on down the spiral of insolvency. The fundamental remedy for rising costs due to inflation is technological improvement, and the usual remedy for rising costs due to government intervention is lobbying, but these measures are not necessarily effective. The liberal arts college cannot introduce much technological improvement without changing its institutional character and losing much of its remaining clientele, and the manufacturers of table linen can bring only a limited influence to bear on government policy.

DECLINING REVENUES

Declining revenues have much the same effect as rising costs, but in the typical case they are a little more under the organization's control, since the decline can sometimes be arrested by vigorous cultivation of an existing clientele or by reaching out for new clients. Advertising and promotion offer the commercial enterprise innumerable opportunities to turn declining sales trends around. Intelligent programs of attracting students enable some liberal arts colleges to flourish when most liberal arts colleges are declining. Hospitals, churches, schools, clubs, civic associations, and innumerable other organizations that depend on voluntary support are often able to reverse a declining revenue trend by intensive cultivation of their existing constituencies, or by reaching out for new supporters.

When we observe the actual behavior of organizations responding to market pressure, we discover that they often act in such a way as to aggravate their initial problems, although there is a pattern of appropriate response to market pressures.[4]

1. *Remember that no trend lasts forever.* The time of peace is the time to prepare for war, and the time of organizational growth is the time to plan and prepare for an inevitable phase of organizational decline.

2. *Every technological improvement should be justified by cost reduction.* Technological improvements are possible in nearly every organized human activity, but since it is also possible to burden nearly any activity with new devices that are not really needed, a technological improvement should not ordinarily be adopted unless it meets the test of appropriateness by offering a significant reduction of cost.

3. *Make multiple responses to market pressure whenever possible, and determine by trial and error which responses are most effective.* An organization's response to market pressure is affected not only by unpredictable fluctuations of the market but also by the responses of competitors, the ramifications elsewhere in the external environment, and the working out of internal stresses. This field of action resembles a storm at sea more than it resembles an acre to be plowed and planted. To get through it safely, you

need to stand by your instruments, take continuous readings, and be prepared to change course when necessary.

Adjusting to social change

No organization can be completely insulated from the currents of social change in the surrounding society. And all societies change continually—not only advanced, industrial societies but *all* societies. The changes that occur in our own society can be classified in many different ways, but those that have the most impact on organizations fall conveniently into four categories: demographic shifts, changes of public policy, changes in social values, and changes in organizational styles.

DEMOGRAPHIC SHIFTS

Demographic shifts occur because of the growth or decline of population in a given territory, or changing rates of growth or decline; because of migration from country to city, from central city to suburb, and from region to region; because of fluctuations in birthrates, death rates, and other vital statistics; and because of changes in the age, sex, ethnicity, and other characteristics of given populations induced by all of the foregoing processes.

Every demographic shift has some effect on organizations, and some of these effects ripple on for decades. For example, the rise in the United States birth rate that occurred in the late 1940s necessitated a great expansion of elementary schools in the 1950s, of high schools a little later, and of colleges and universities in the 1960s. The sharp decline of the same birthrate that occurred in the 1970s calls for a shrinkage of educatirnal institutions tha+ will continue until the end of the century.

To take another familiar example, the great, predominantly white migrations of urban dwellers to the suburbs that take place periodically have profound effects upon the city churches they formerly attended, which respond to the problem of declining attendance and interest in a variety of ways. Some urban churches follow their congregations to the suburbs. Some continue to operate on a much reduced scale for a remnant of elderly parishioners, some go out of existence, and some reorganize to serve a new clientele.

No national population in the modern world has a fixed size, distribution, or composition; all of them are continuously changing. Hence, all modern organizations are subject to continuous demographic shifts that determine the number and type of persons eligible for involvement in their programs.

CHANGES OF PUBLIC POLICY

Changes in public policy have frequent and unpredictable effects upon organizations of every kind in every modern society. In the People's Democracies (and under some other dictatorial governments), no aspect of organizational life falls outside the sphere of official control. Under a freer form of government, the jurisdiction of the state is more limited but constantly expanding. The expenditures of all levels of government in the United States account for more than a third of the gross national product, while governmental control over nongovernmental organizations is steadily extended by an unending stream of statutes, regulations, and rulings emitted by legislatures, courts, and administrative agencies. Even an isolated organization, such as a private fishing club, must file a tax statement, apply for licenses, conform to health, safety, and zoning regulations, pay minimum wages, refrain from illegal discrimination, operate equipment in a prescribed manner, and so on and so forth. An establishment of a more public character, such as a hotel or a hospital, operates within an intricate maze of government controls.

There are hundreds of separate government bodies with the power to alter some of the public policies that control the operation of a hospital, and many of them are hyperactive in developing new policies and procedures. For example, in the reimbursement of hospitals from public funds for charges incurred by indigent patients, about the only thing that can be taken for granted concerning the policies and procedures in effect at a given time is that they will be different twelve months later.

A statute or court ruling intended to accomplish some unrelated purpose may transform an organization's environment beyond recognition, as has repeatedly happened in recent years to organizations as diverse as nursery schools, nursing homes, and tree nurseries, within my own observation. In the case of the nursery schools, a careless phrase in a state law on the licensing of schoolteachers had the effect of requiring nursery schoolteachers to have bachelor's degrees in education, thereby eliminating a good proportion of the nursery schools in that state and tripling or quadrupling the average charges of those that remained. In the case of nursing homes, a small change in the regulations concerning Medicare eligibility forced many large nursing homes to dismantle their facilities for intensive medical care. In the case of the tree nurseries, a minor revision in the federal tax regulations concerning depletion allowances made Christmas tree nurseries highly attractive to investors at one time, while another minor revision some years later made them instantly unprofitable.

The realm of public policy constitutes a Pandora's box of unexpected surprises, sometimes pleasant but more often unpleasant for the modern organization. Nearly every sizable organization is continually engaged in lobbying and litigation, either directly or through representative associations. Nevertheless, since changes in public policy come from so many different quarters, an organization will often be unaware that some significant modification is about to be required in its program until the change is upon it. For example, the Buckley amendment requiring educational institutions to give students access to all confidential records about themselves, which transformed the record-keeping procedures of educational institutions, was enacted and took effect before the affected institutions or their official lobbyists were aware that such a measure was impending.

CHANGES IN SOCIAL VALUES

Changes in social values are even more unpredictable in the long run than changes in public policy, but since they are much less abrupt, they permit more intelligent planning and adaptation. Changes in social values involve such matters as the relationship between the sexes, the attitudes of young people toward their elders, the limits of legitimate authority, the recognition or denial of property rights, the importance attached to education and to leisure, the role of religion in daily life, the tolerance accorded to people of different color or descent, and the definition of what constitutes acceptable appearance, speech, and behavior in various settings. No organization is impermeable to changes in social values, but most organizations do not absorb such changes passively; they either encourage or resist them. With respect to such a matter as the equalization of sex roles, a strong organization is likely to be either far ahead of, or far behind, the general social trend. Few organizations, however, remain unaffected.

The movement that developed in the late 1960s to equalize the treatment of the sexes in the United States was reflected in the campaign for the Equal Rights Amendment, the literature of the women's liberation movement, a long series of rulings by federal and state courts invalidating established forms of differentiation by sex, and the establishment of a new federal agency, the Equal Employment Opportunity Commission, with specific powers to enforce equal opportunity and equal pay for women workers.

Needless to say, these changes were embedded in the larger context of changes in sexual relationships inside and outside the family. Public policy and public opinion combined to force nearly every all-male organization to admit women and, with much less insistence, to encourage all-female organizations to admit men. In many organizations, such as boarding schools and prisons, this involved profound transformations. In other organizations, such as men's bars, craft unions, and naval vessels, the token admission of a few women had more symbolic than practical effect.

CHANGES IN ORGANIZATIONAL STYLES

Organizational styles change as frequently as styles in clothing or entertainment. Fashions and fads in organizational matters are partly derived from the external environment and partly self-generated. Modern organizations of a given type are in much closer touch with one another nowadays than formerly, through conventions and a vast flow of periodicals, so that any significant innovation in an organization is noticed almost immediately by other organizations in the same set, and any innovation that has been adopted by a number of organizations becomes almost irresistible to others. Where formerly there were high barriers between Christian denominations, for example, there is now such easy and natural communication among them that the modernization of the liturgy of the mass in Roman Catholic churches impelled many Protestant churches to revise their liturgies in a similar fashion.

When an organization is confronted with an external social change that invites or compels action, the manager ought to be mindful of the following:

1. *Do not be taken unaware.* It is the manager's personal responsibility to be aware of changes in the external environment that affect the organization's program, and this responsibility can never really be delegated.

2. *Do not allow the organization to react hastily.* The problems of adjusting an organization to externally imposed change are inherently complex, and the probability of finding the right solution by intuition is necessarily low.

3. *Determine the objectives to be achieved and then work backward step by step to find the appropriate means.* This is known as the sequential approach to problem solving, and I have discussed it in detail in another book.[5]

4. *Make sure that you have a substantial consensus within the organization before responding to external changes.* The existence of a consensus is ascertained by consultation with the people directly or indirectly affected by the proposed course of action. If there is no consensus, it must be developed by having the same people study the problem until they arrive at agreement or, in extreme circumstances, by a drastic reorganization in favor of one faction. How much consensus is enough is always a good question, but it is easy to underestimate the resistance to change that can be mustered by a disgruntled minority, or by the one wicked witch not invited to the christening.

5. *When following organizational fashions, do not be the last with the old nor the first with the new.* This is an old doctor's adage concerning the application of new remedies. It rests on the commonsense observations that the first users of a new remedy are the ones most likely to suffer from its unknown side effects, while the last users have the least profit from its benefits.

Adjusting to technological progress

In an advanced technological society, all organizations, including those that have nothing to do with industrial production, are offered a continuous stream of technologically improved devices. The museum of antique furniture is offered a computerized catalog system. The rowing club can pace its practice sessions with an electronically activated timer, whether or not it has already changed from wooden to fiberglass oars.

Technological progress involves mechanization, automatization, cybernation, and progressive increases in the efficiency of each of these processes by means of improved materials and more sophisticated mechanisms.

From the technological standpoint, an improvement is an improvement; even the casual observer can usually determine which of two related devices is more advanced along the vector of technological progress. But the problem of whether an organization needs, wants, or can make use of a given bit of new technology is not so easily resolved. It is possible to automate a dairy farm so that the cows are fed and milked without any human intervention, but it is not economically practical to do so except with a very large herd.

From the organizational standpoint, technological improvement usually involves both advantages and disadvantages. The advantages are usually along the lines of greater speed, scope, capacity, and precision and (sometimes) lower unit costs. The disadvantages are along the lines of the loss of autonomy, waste of skills, reduction in cooperative effort, decreased control, and (sometimes) increased unit costs.

Hence, the adjustment of an organization to technological progress in its field involves two separate tasks: first, choosing or rejecting new technological improvements as they are offered; second, incorporating whatever improvements are chosen into the organizational program with minimum damage. In many technically oriented organizations, there is the third task of contributing to the development of new technology by research and experimentation. Let us consider the first two tasks first. The third falls under the heading of creative innovation and will be taken up in the next section.

CHOOSING OR REJECTING NEW TECHNOLOGY

This task is more of a pitfall for small organizations than for large ones. Large organizations, with their specialized technical facilities, participate directly in the current of ongoing research and usually have reasonable procedures for appraising the advantages and disadvantages of a proposed bit of new technology. There are some notable exceptions, however. The United States Post Office, for example, has so powerful a tradition of technological ineptness that private message and parcel services are able to compete with it effectively, despite the enormous subsidy it enjoys.

In any case, the rules of thumb for choosing or rejecting a new bit of technology are the same for organizations of every size. They may be stated as follows:

1. Adopt a technological improvement when it offers a large and unmistakable reduction of cost or gain of efficacy, or both.

2. Reject a technological improvement when its costs or its efficacy are uncertain.

3. Adopt a technological improvement if it can be introduced on an experimental basis without serious jeopardy to the organizational program in case of failure.

4. Reject a technological improvement that exposes the organization to disaster in certain contingencies such as the disappearance of a supplier or the displacement of the proposed new technology by a still more advanced technology.

INCORPORATING NEW TECHNOLOGY INTO AN ORGANIZATION

The decision to adopt a new bit of technology is frequently made at the top level of an organization (or by outsiders, in the case of organizations that are components of larger ones) without any serious attention to the problem of fitting the innovation into the organization. That is where the sociological fun begins.

The installation of a new bit of technology in an organization often bears some resemblance to the modernization of a primitive village by well-meaning outside experts. The things that can go wrong because the experts fail to take full account of the habits, customs, and beliefs of the people and the conditions in which they live were admirably cataloged by Conrad Arensberg and Arthur Niehoff in the manual they prepared for American experts working overseas.

They had many anecdotes to tell about misdirected technological improvements; for example, in Laotian villages, Leghorn and Rhode Island Red roosters were put into village flocks to raise a more productive mixed breed:

> Some American chickens survived but even these got no chance to prove their usefulness. They rarely were able to mate with the local hens because they were no match for the gamecocks that served as roosters in the local flocks. The chicken expert tried to get around this difficulty by demanding that a villager get rid of all of his local roosters before he would put some American ones in the flock. This worked for one generation. Then the sons of the American roosters and the Lao hens took over. Being half village chicken, they were tougher fighters than their fathers, and kept the latter from mating. In this manner, each generation became inferior in size and egg-producing ability, but superior in fighting.[6]

The reason that the American expert could not overcome these difficulties was that he never fully visualized the difference between the American system of raising chickens in a tightly controlled hen house environment and the Laotian system of letting the chickens forage for themselves, nor did he perceive the connection between the local sport of cock-fighting and poultry husbandry.

Exactly the same sort of incomprehension often attends the introduction of a technological innovation in a sophisticated enterprise. A textbook publisher who installed an automated shipping system in a computerized warehouse discovered that his salesmen were ordering out huge numbers of examination copies under fictitious names and hoarding them. The new system, it turned out, had an average delivery time of around fifteen days, much less than that of the previous system; but, unlike the previous system, it was incapable of delivering a book overnight on a salesman's rush order. Since the salesman depended on such rush orders whenever a buyer showed interest, they bypassed the new warehouse and improvised a makeshift system of their own in order to get their work done.

What appears to be an irrational resistance to technology often turns out, in closer analysis, to be rational enough from the standpoint of the resisters. The Lancaster weavers who smashed the power looms at the very beginning of the Industrial Revolution feared that their wages would be lowered by the new invention and, in fact, they were perfectly right.

Even when the resistance to an invention is irrational, it may be quite reasonable in terms of the information available to the resisters. The fault in such cases lies with the innovators for not having sufficiently studied the environment in which they proposed to operate.

To take another example from the modernization of developing countries, the team of agronomists from the University of Iowa who attempted to introduce an improved variety of seed corn in highland Guatemala discovered that although the local farmers took the corn gratefully enough, they fed it to their animals instead of planting it. After two or three seasons of this charade, the agronomists, on the advice of an astute Indian, put a high fence studded with No Trespassing signs around their compound and stopped giving their seed corn away. But they left the fence unguarded at night and enough corn was stolen and planted to establish the new variety. In that part of the world, nearly every family has its own subvariety of corn, and it is much too valuable to give away. But if it appears really superior, the neighbors are not above pilfering some to try out.

The first series of experiments at the Western Electric plant in Hawthorne nearly half a century ago, which had such a profound effect on the development of industrial sociology, attempted to demonstrate the effect of improved lighting on the productivity of factory work groups. In one of these experiments, a test group was chosen to work under progressively improving illumination. It was carefully matched with a control group, working under constant illumination. The results were startling. The increase of productivity in the control group was nearly the same as the increase in the experimental group. In a follow-up experiment, both the test group and the control group were placed in artificial light, and this time the level of illumination in the test group enclosure was gradually decreased. Again, the efficiencies of the test group and the control group increased at about the same rate. Not until the test group's illumination was reduced to the approximate brightness of moonlight, so that they could barely see their materials, did output begin to decrease.

The implication of this experiment was that the level of illumination had only a minor influence on productivity in that particular setting, but that the amount of supervisory attention received by a work group had a major influence. Both the test group and the control group were closely watched, fussed over, and consulted by supervisors during the course of the experiment; the favorable effects of this increased attention seemed to overcome the minor effects of varying illumination.

In general, the successful introduction of a technological innovation depends upon predicting with reasonable accuracy (1) what functions the innovation will perform and how these will affect the organization's structure, and (2) obtaining—preferably in advance—the consent and cooperation of the people who are expected to make the innovation work.

The usual procedures for accomplishing these purposes may be summarized as follows:

1. Before committing the organization to a technological innovation, it is essential to obtain empirical evidence that the innovation is workable, by means of a pilot installation or by close observation of a comparable organization in which it is already operational.

2. The more people involved in preliminary discussion of, and planning for, the innovation, the more successful it is likely to be.

3. When resistance to an innovation begins to develop, stop the clock and resolve the problem before proceeding further. Resistance of this kind should not be approached as an obstacle to be surmounted. It may be solidly grounded on technical or social factors that deserve to be taken into account.

4. Try to determine in advance, primarily by consultation outside and inside the organization, the probable defects of a proposed innovation so as to be prepared to cope with them as they appear.

5. A technological innovation should be monitored for a considerable period of time after its installation in order to detect those malfunctions that take some time to develop and in order to measure the results of the innovation when it settles into a steady state of operation.

Creative innovation

March and Simon, in their classic treatise on the theory of organization, hypothesize that "most innovations in an organization are a result of borrowing rather than invention."[7] The borrowing is accomplished either by direct imitation of other organizations or by importing people who have experience elsewhere. The practice of borrowing makes eminent good sense, particularly for small organizations, since the borrower is spared the cost of invention and testing and is protected to a considerable extent from the errors of trial-and-error experimentation.

Nevertheless, any organization may occasionally engage in independent invention and produce a new technical or social device, and some organizations and branches of organizations are in the business of inventing such devices. This activity currently goes by the somewhat pretentious name of creative innovation and is undertaken with varying degrees of seriousness in scientific laboratories, research and development teams, advertising agencies, law firms, and a few high-level planning agencies.

Under primitive conditions, creative innovation is the exclusive prerogative of a few individuals who have the rare talent of perceiving connections and possibilities to which their fellows are blind. While filming the lives of monkeys (red-faced macaques) on the island of Kochima, a team of Japanese zoologists actually saw a young female (whom they nicknamed Imo) hit on the idea of washing a sweet potato in the lake before eating it. After about a month, she was imitated by another monkey, and ten years later, the practice had spread throughout the band. Later, Imo made a second fundamental discovery when she hit on a method of separating grain from sand by tossing a pawful of grain on the surface of the water and letting the sand sink. "She was something of a monkey Prometheus," wrote one observer.[8]

The characteristics of inventive geniuses do not change very much as we ascend the evolutionary scale. They are rare, conscious of their special gifts, and capable of making multiple discoveries when given the right conditions.

Creative innovators seem to have distinctive mental and personality traits. They rate high on conceptual fluency and flexibility, respond to stimuli in original and atypical ways, and enjoy complex problems. They are likely to be stubborn about their opinions, somewhat lonely, impulsive, and resistant to authority. In other words, they are almost the antithesis of conventional organization men.[9]

The problem of designing an organization to encourage and facilitate creative innovation is challenging, and, in the present state of knowledge, it cannot be answered by a simple formula. There is considerable disagreement among successful research administrators about how much autonomy the creative innovator needs to have. The question is complicated by the fact that in contemporary science, technology, and social management, the problems to be solved by creative innovation sometimes call for a massive team effort. The individual capable of original discoveries does not lose his importance, but his work must now be coordinated with the less original efforts of numerous hardworking collaborators.

The available research evidence suggests that administrative style, tables of organization, and operating procedures are less important in creative organizations than in those with more routine programs. The most productive research organization I have ever observed was Millard Hansen's Social Science Research Center at the University of Puerto Rico—although it was enmeshed in the toils of an old-fashioned, slow-moving, bilingual bureaucracy. The secret of the center's success seems to have been that project directors were very carefully selected and then given unlimited responsibility for their projects and as much support as the center could provide with no questions asked and no reports required between the launching of a project and its completion two to ten years later. The classic example and prototype of the American industrial laboratory, the research division of General Electric under Irving Langmuir, operated in a similar fashion.

On the other hand, the two greatest achievements of American technology, the Manhattan project and the NASA moon program, were carried out by tightly administered organizations, each of which had a rather narrow and rigid division of labor. In contrast to the absence of deadlines in Hansen's center and Langmuir's laboratory (other than those self-imposed by individuals), some effective research organizations not only impose deadlines but have on occasion used the trick of a suddenly advanced deadline to achieve a breakthrough on a stubborn problem.

While the optimum design for a creative organization cannot be completely specified, there are a few well-established principles for managing a creative organization, which may be stated as follows:

1. Identify the creative individuals on whom the success of the organization depends, on the basis of their demonstrated performance.

2. Make sure that you and they share a common view of the organization's purposes, whether broadly or narrowly defined.

3. Provide them with all the support the organization can muster.

4. Protect them from bureaucratic interference.

5. Reward them as lavishly as possible.

It is obvious from the foregoing that the noncreative people in a creative organization will suffer from relative deprivation, and that the creative people will sometimes get in each other's way. Successful research organizations are seldom characterized by high morale, but that matters little if they are able to produce original discoveries and new ideas.

Systematic planning

The reader, if he has any organizational experience at all, will not have needed this book to tell him that management is more an art than a science, although the findings of social science may assist us in practicing the art. He would not have needed a book, either, to tell him that both pleasures and pains are associated with the headship of anything. "Is it not passing brave to be a King and ride in triumph through Persepolis," wrote Christopher Marlowe in *Tamburlaine,* but "uneasy lies the head that wears a crown," wrote his greater contemporary in *Henry IV.*

The principles of conduct proposed in the foregoing pages can be read backward as signposts pointing toward the pitfalls into which a manager can fall, and sometimes must fall. The balance between success and failure in running an organization is so delicate that common sense tells us to count no manager successful until he has retired and gone away.

Is there some sure method of tipping this uncertain balance in our favor? The answer is *no* if we want to be guaranteed against unknown dangers, unprovoked hostility, and the consequences of our own mistakes. The answer is *yes* if we want to improve an organization by maintaining authority, encouraging communication, achieving high levels of productivity and morale, and adapting successfully to change. A nearly magical enhancement of the manager's personal capability can be achieved nine times out of ten by an intelligent emphasis on planning.

In nearly every kind of organization, the manager has a primary responsibility for the planning function not likely to be questioned or disputed. Even a manager with very limited authority, such as the principal of a public school or the president of a civic association, is usually free to launch as much planning activity as he wishes and can usually enlist participants in a planning program without meeting much resistance.

Planning may, of course, be short-term, middle-term, or long-term; routine or episodic; problem-oriented or goal-oriented, participant or nonparticipant. But the essential features of a well-conceived planning program are not very much affected by these distinctions.

Not all of what passes for organizational planning deserves the name. Some so-called plans are really sales prospectuses. Others are science fiction. In a few interesting cases, the sole function of planning is to direct attention away from current problems.

Serious planning, by contrast, is marked by an emphasis on contingency and by a meticulous interest in small details. The minimum essential elements of a serious plan are:

1. A detailed description of the current state of the organization and of the relevant features of its environment.

2. An analysis of past trends in the organization and in the environment to provide a basis for extrapolating the same trends into the future.

3. A division of the future into successive stages and a description of the conditions to be achieved at each stage.

4. Estimates of the organizational inputs required to move from the present through the progressive stages of the planned future.

5. Specification of the external condition required to carry the plan through its successive stages.

6. Methods for measuring plan fulfillment at successive stages.

7. Provisions for revising the plan in case of overfulfillment, underfulfillment, or other unforeseeable contingencies.

The direct advantages of planning are obvious. The indirect benefits are not quite so obvious but they are equally real and just as important.

SELF-APPRAISAL

In organizations that practice continuous short-term planning, for example in companies that set production or sales quotas for six months or a year ahead, the pressures for achievement on the one hand, and the politics of quota-setting on the other hand, force every unit of the organization—down to the individual worker—to practice continuous self-appraisal. In middle- and long-term planning, a major planning episode usually begins with a self-survey in which units assess their past progress, present performance, and potential capability in relation to the organization's stated goals. This experience, repeated at reasonable intervals and in a reasonably democratic spirit, has all sorts of wonderful side effects. It is by far the most effective way of clarifying the organization's goals and bringing the activities of component units into alignment with them. It leads units to uncover and resolve many structural and operating problems that would otherwise go untreated. It elicits information and suggestions from parts of the organization that do not normally play much part in formulating policy, while the need to combine the reports of lower units at each level provokes intense communication—upward, downward, and sideways—about organizational problems.[10]

CLARIFICATION OF GOALS

No matter how clearly the initial goals of an organization are stated or understood, some ambiguities, differences of opinion, and misunderstandings are sure to develop in the course of normal operations, with the result that one part of the program pulls against another, or some units spend their energies undoing the work of other units. Planning brings these contradictions to light and provides incentives to resolve them, at least within the confines of the plan.

NEW POSSIBILITIES

Part of the magic of planning is the almost inevitable discovery of possible courses of action not previously imagined or noticed. The simple procedure of arranging alternatives and contingencies in an orderly way often leads to useful new strategies that would never have otherwise suggested themselves.

IMPROVED INFORMATION

Nearly the first thing that happens in the preparation of an organizational plan is that people find they need information that is not readily available, either because the reporting system is not set up to deliver it, or because it has not been collected, or because it needs to be obtained from outside the organization. When the reporting system has been modified to produce the needed information, or channels to outside sources of information have been established, there is likely to be a marked improvement in the information routinely gathered afterward.

HOW NOT TO PLAN

Planning, like any other magic, can turn against its user. The failures of planning loom so large in the current world that they deserve separate consideration. Defective planning is one of the hallmarks of modern bureaucracy, and takes several familiar forms:

1. *Setting organizational objectives without participation and consent.* This is the characteristic form of planning in the Soviet economy and, to a lesser extent, in the other centralized economies of eastern Europe. It is one of the principal reasons why their productivity lags so far behind that of the partially planned economies of western Europe, despite the advantage of more tightly disciplined labor forces in the eastern countries.

2. *Planning with unlimited resources.* The whole point of planning is that it enables an organization to adjust its program to existing constraints in a realistic way. Limited resources constitute a fundamental constraint in most cases. If, for some reason, the resources potentially available to an organization are limited only by its demands, there will be a tendency to plan for maximum growth rather than maximum effectiveness. This is a common occurrence in government agencies since they draw on resources that, at least in the short and middle term, are virtually unlimited. It occurs also in some private organizations whose budgets are so small in relation to the sources from which they draw support as to be practically unlimited. For example, the private security forces of large private institutions seem to develop in a less effective way when planned than when unplanned, since the planning of security services is conventionally oriented toward expansion rather than efficiency.

3. *Master planning.* Master planning is an aberration of the planning process to which American communities are particularly susceptible. The preparation of a master plan is a gigantic effort, altogether out of scale with routine planning activities. The typical master plan is not a statement of intentions but a mixture of practical possibilities and pious hopes that refer to some future time too remote to be controlled from the present. In many cases, the master plan takes so long to prepare that it is outdated before it is published. Master plans seldom specify intermediate stages in detail and, because of their gigantic scale, are not easily amended to take account of intervening events. But the overhanging presence of a master plan has a tendency to inhibit or interfere with realistic planning on a smaller scale.

4. *Planning by outsiders.* It is a common practice for large-scale organizations of every kind to bring in outside experts to do their long-term planning. In some instances where the plan involves very little besides the installation of a new technology, as in the construction of a water purification plant, this procedure makes sense. In the more usual situation, in which modifications in the structure or functions of a living organization are contemplated, it is nearly impossible for outsiders to plan effectively, however knowledgeable and experienced they may be. Consultants are useful to get the planning process going, to suggest new methods and new systems, and to carry styles of self-improvement from one organization to another; but they cannot successfully plan the future of an organization to which they do not belong. That is the inherent responsibility of the organization's active members. Without their consent and participation, planning is a hollow show.

Phasing yourself out

Involvement in long-term planning serves to remind a manager that his tenure of office will not be eternal and forces him to consider the relationship between his policies and those of his successor, a subject he might otherwise be tempted to overlook.

In very large organizations, the problem of arranging an orderly succession, and of striking a balance between the continuity of policy that is so desirable and the fresh start that every successor is entitled to make, is not likely to be overlooked. A report on the General Electric company states somewhat breathlessly that the chief operating executive "keeps current a list of five potential successors for his job." But in organizations of a more modest scale, and in the many large organizations that operate under the lengthened shadow of one leader, the questions associated with succession commonly come under a kind of primitive taboo. As in some African tribes, he who mentions the death of the chief is suspected of working to bring it about.

Aside from dispelling this taboo, which is in every way unwholesome, the manager who plans his own succession is certain to discover that more is involved than finding a younger man or woman with big enough feet to fill his hulking shoes. In nearly every organization, it is part of his managerial responsibility to assure that such a person, or two or three of them, will be available when the time comes, and doing so requires some restructuring of the current program.

In many instances, he will be led to the further discovery that the most effective transition would be gradual and that the selection of a successor ought to take place before—in some cases long before—his own retirement.

The manager who gives serious consideration to the problem of how to establish his successor's authority on a firm basis has come full circle and finds himself again confronting the problem with which he started. If he gets that far without cynicism or remorse, he and the organization will have done very well by each other.

Notes

Chapter 1

1. For other elements of the pattern, see Oscar Grusky, "The effects of succession: a comparative study of military and business organization," in Oscar Grusky and George A. Miller, eds., *The Sociology of Organizations: Basic Studies* (New York: Free Press, 1970), pp. 439–61.

2. Donald B. Trow, "Executive Succession in Small Companies," *Administrative Science Quarterly* 6, no. 2 (September 1961): 237–39.

3. Alvin W. Gouldner, *Patterns of Industrial Bureaucracy* (Glencoe, Ill.: Free Press, 1954), especially pp. 70–101.

4. Robert H. Guest, *Organizational Change: The Effect of Successful Leadership* (Homewood, Ill.: Irwin-Dorsey, 1962).

5. Edmund P. Learned and Audrey T. Sproat, *Organization Theory and Policy: Notes for Analysis* (Homewood, Ill.: Richard D. Irwin, Inc., 1966).

6. Michel Crozier, *The Bureaucratic Phenomenon* (Chicago: University of Chicago Press, 1964), pp. 113–14.

7. Rensis Likert, *New Patterns of Management* (New York: McGraw-Hill, 1961).

8. Peter Drucker, *The Practice of Management* (New York: Harper and Brothers, 1954).

9. Georges Friedmann, *Le Travail en Miettes* (Paris: Gallimard, 1956).

10. The story of this development is told in "Pioneers in Industrial Sociology," in John Madge, *The Origins of Scientific Sociology* (Glencoe, Ill.: Free Press, 1962), pp. 162–209.

11. Elliott Jaques, *The Changing Culture of a Factory* (New York: Dryden Press, 1952), p. 277.

12. Gordon Tullock, *The Politics of Bureaucracy* (Washington, D.C.: Public Affairs Press, 1965), p. 179.

13. Antony Jay, *Management and Machiavelli: An Inquiry into Politics of Corporate Life* (New York: Holt, Rinehart and Winston, 1968), p. 38.

14. William Foote Whyte, *Street Corner Society: The Social Structure of an Italian Slum* (Chicago: University of Chicago Press, 1943).

15. Ervin Goffman, *Relations in Public: Microstudies of the Public Order* (New York: Basic Books, 1971).

16. Reece M. McGee, "A Study in Ambience: The Numerical Analysis of Interaction Groupings in a Large Scale Organization" (Ph.D. diss., University of Minnesota, 1956).

17. Theodore Caplow, *Two Against One: Coalitions in Triads* (Englewood Cliffs, N.J.: Prentice-Hall, 1968).

18. Georg Simmel, *The Sociology of Georg Simmel*, trans. Kurt H. Wolff (Glencoe, Ill.: Free Press, 1950), pp. 165–66.

19. Theodore C. Sorensen, *Kennedy* (New York: Harper and Row, 1965), pp. 679 ff.

Chapter 2

1. Chester I. Barnard, *The Functions of the Executive* (Cambridge, Mass.: Harvard University Press, 1938).

2. Stanley E. Seashore and Ephraim Yuchtman, "The Elements of Organizational Performance," in Bernard P. Indik and F. Kenneth Berrien, eds., *People, Groups, and Organizations* (New York: Teachers College Press, 1968), pp. 172–88.

3. Donald Roy, "Efficiency and 'The Fix': Informal Intergroup Relations in a Piecework Machine Shop," *American Journal of Sociology* 60, no. 3 (November 1954), pp. 255–66.

4. Howard Guetzkow et al., *Simulation in International Relations* (Englewood Cliffs, N.J.: Prentice-Hall, 1963).

5. James David Barber, *Power in Committees: An Experiment in the Governmental Process* (Chicago: Rand-McNally, 1966).

6. Richard F. Fenno, Jr., "The House Appropriations Committee as a Political System: The Problem of Integration," *American Political Science Review* 66 (1962): 310–24.

7. Leonard Berkowitz, "Group standards, cohesiveness and productivity," *Human Relations* 7, no. 4 (1954): 509–19.

8. F. J. Roethlisberger and William J. Dickson (with Harold A. Wright), *Management and the Worker* (Cambridge, Mass.: Harvard University Press, 1939).

9. A. J. M. Sykes, "A Study in Changing the Attitudes and Stereotypes of Industrial Workers," *Human Relations* 17, no. 2 (1964).

10. Rensis Likert, *New Patterns of Management* (New York: McGraw-Hill, 1961).

11. Stephen A. Richardson, "Organization Contrasts on British and American Ships," *Administrative Science Quarterly* (September 1956). A more detailed description of the British arrangement may be found in Peter H. Fricke, *The Social Structure of Crews* . . . (Durham, Wales: University of Wales, Department of Maritime Studies, 1974).

12. The range of ulterior motives for hiring consultants is described in a brilliant chapter on "The Advice Market" in Wilbert E. Moore, *The Conduct of the Corporation* (New York: Random House, 1962).

13. Edmond Cahn, *The Predicament of Democratic Man* (New York: Macmillan, 1961), pp. 178–80.

14. See the section on rumor in Gardner Lindzey and Elliot Aronson, eds., *The Handbook of Social Psychology*, 2nd ed. (Reading, Mass.: Addison-Wesley, 1969).

15. Daniel Katz, "Approaches to Managing Conflict," in Robert L. Kahan and Elise Boulding, eds., *Power and Conflict in Organizations* (New York: Basic Books, 1964).

16. David Riesman, Nathan Glazer, and Reuel Denney, *The Lonely Crowd* (Garden City, N.Y.: Doubleday Anchor Books, 1953), pp. 243–45.

Chapter 3

1. David M. Ogilvy, "The Creative Chef," in G. A. Steiner, ed., *The Creative Organization* (Chicago: University of Chicago Press, 1965), p. 202.

2. Ibid., p. 203.

3. Alfred Chandler, "Strategy and Structure: The Sloan Structure of General Motors," reprinted in M. W. Meyer, ed., *Structures, Symbols and Systems* (Boston: Little, Brown, 1971).

4. Ibid., p. 354.

5. Frederick W. Taylor, "Scientific Management," reprinted in Grusky and Miller, eds., *The Sociology of Organizations: Basic Studies* (New York: Free Press, 1970), p. 49.

6. Ibid., p. 51.

7. Elton Mayo, *Human Problems of an Industrial Civilization* (New York: Macmillan, 1933); and Fritz J. Roethlisberger and William J. Dickson, *Management and the Worker* (Cambridge, Mass.: Harvard University Press, 1939).

8. Rensis Likert, *New Patterns of Management* (New York: McGraw-Hill, 1961).

9. Melville Dalton, "Managing the Managers," *Human Organization* 14, no. 3 (Fall 1955): 410.

10. Joseph Bensman and Israel Gerver, "Crime and Punishment in the Factory: The Function of Deviancy in Maintaining the Social System," in J. M. Shepard, ed., *Organizational Issues in Industrial Society* (Englewood Cliffs, N.J.: Prentice-Hall, 1972), pp. 181–95.

11. Adapted from Frank Pieper, *Modular Management and Human Leadership* (Minneapolis: Methods Press, 1958), pp. 69–70.

12. Summarized in Bernard M. Bass and Gerald V. Barrett, *Man, Work and Organization* (Boston: Allyn and Bacon, 1972) p. 58.

13. For an interesting case history, see Dalton, "Managing the Managers," pp. 139–41.

14. Joseph S. Berliner, "A Problem in Soviet Business Administration," reprinted in Oscar Grusky and George A. Miller, eds., *The Sociology of Organizations: Basic Studies* (New York: Free Press, 1970), p. 561.

15. Peter M. Blau, *The Dynamics of Bureaucracy*, rev. ed. (Chicago: University of Chicago Press, 1963).

Chapter 4

1. Roy Lewis and Rosemary Stewart, *The Managers: A New Examination of the English, German and American Executive* (New York: Mentor Books, 1961), pp. 73–74.

2. Barbara M. Korsch and Vida Francis Negrete, "Doctor-Patient Communication," *Scientific American* 227 (August 1972): 66–74.

3. Sanford N. Dornbusch, "The Military Academy as an Assimilat-

ing Institution," *Social Forces* 33, no. 4 (May 1955), pp. 316–21.

4. Harry Levenson, *Organizational Diagnosis* (Cambridge, Mass.: Harvard University Press, 1972), p. 411.

5. C. H. Lawshe and A. D. McGinley, "Job performance criteria studies I. The job performance of proofreaders," *Journal of Applied Psychology* 35 (1951): 316–20.

6. John C. Flanagan and Robert K. Burns, "The Employee Performance Record: A New Appraisal and Development Tool," *Harvard Business Review* 33, no. 5 (September-October 1955): 95.

7. See J. Stacy Adams, "Inequity in Social Exchange," in L. Berkowitz, ed., *Advances in Experimental Social Psychology* (New York: Academic Press, 1965), pp. 265–99; and George C. Homans, *Social Behavior: Its Elementary Forms* (New York: Harcourt Brace, 1961).

8. J. Berger et al., *Distributive Justice: A Status Value Formulation*, Stanford University Technical Report no. 28 (Stanford, Calif., 1968).

9. For a spectacular example, see Landon Y. Jones, Jr., "Bad Days on Mount Olympus: The Big Shoot-out at the Institute for Advanced Study," *Atlantic* 233, no. 2 (February 1974): 37–53.

10. Samuel A. Stouffer et al., *Studies in Social Psychology in World War II*, 4 vols. (Princeton, N.J.: Princeton University Press, 1949–50).

11. This situation, as actually observed, is described in Peter H. Fricke, *The Social Structure of Crews . . .* (Durham, Wales: University of Wales, Department of Maritime Studies, 1974).

12. Herbert A. Shepard, "Responses to Situations of Competition in Conflict," in Robert L. Cahn and Elise Boulding, *Power and Conflict in Organizations* (New York: Basic Books, 1964), pp. 130–33.

13. Orvis Collins, "Ethnic Behavior in Industry: Sponsorship and Rejection in a New England Factory," *American Journal of Sociology* 51 (January 1946): 293–98

Chapter 5

1. A full description of team management may be found in Peter H. Drucker, *Management: Tasks, Responsibilities, Practices* (New York: Harper and Row, 1974).

2. Erving Goffman, *Asylums* (New York: Anchor Books, 1961).

3. C. Northcote Parkinson, *Parkinson's Law and Other Studies in Administration* (Boston: Houghton-Mifflin, 1957).

4. Much more information on this topic can be found in Harvey A. Hornstein et al., *Social Intervention: A Behavioral Science Approach* (New York: Free Press, 1971).

5. Theodore Caplow, *Towards Social Hope* (New York: Basic Books, 1975).

6. Conrad N. Arensberg and Arthur H. Niehoff, *Introducing Social Change: A Manual for Americans Overseas* (Chicago: Aldine, 1964), p. 77.

7. James G. March and Herman A. Simon, *Organizations* (New York: John Wiley and Sons, 1958), p. 188.

8. The original observations are somewhat inaccessible, but the film has been widely shown, and a good summary may be found in Vitus B. Droscher, *The Friendly Beast* (New York: Harper and Row, 1971), pp. 191–92.

9. Gary A. Steiner, *The Creative Organization* (Chicago: University of Chicago Press, 1965).

10. Such a situation is described in detail by Neal Gross, Joseph B. Giacquinto, and Marty Bernstein, in *Implementing Organizational Innovations* (New York: Basic Books, 1971).

Reading list on the art of management

Bailey, F. G. *Stratagems and Spoils*. New York: Schocken Books, 1969.

Bass, Bernard M., and Barret, Gerald V. *Man, Work and Organizations*. Boston: Allyn and Bacon, 1972.

Bernard, Chester I. *The Functions of the Executive*. Cambridge, Mass.: Harvard University Press, 1938.

Drucker, Peter F. *Managing for Results*. New York: Harper and Row, 1974.

Jay, Antony. *Management and Machiavelli*. New York: Holt, Rinehart and Winston, 1968.

Krupp, Sherman. *Pattern in Organization Analysis*. New York: Holt, Rinehart and Winston, 1961.

Leavitt, Harold J. et al. *The Organizational World*. New York: Harcourt Brace Jovanovich, 1973.

Likert, Rensis. *New Patterns of Management*. New York: McGraw-Hill, 1961.

Odiorne, George S. *Management and the Activity Trap*. New York: Harper and Row, 1974.

Parkinson, C. Northcote. *In-Laws and Outlaws*. Boston: Houghton-Mifflin, 1962.

Pieper, Frank. *Modular Management and Human Leadership*. Minneapolis: Methods Press, 1958.

Sayles, Leonard R. *Managerial Behavoir*. New York: McGraw-Hill, 1964.

Thompson, James D. *Organizations in Action*. New York: McGraw-Hill, 1967.

Walton, Clarence C. *Ethos and the Executive*. Englewood Cliffs, N.J.: Prentice-Hall, 1969.

Index

Index 219

Organizations, 3; common characteristics, 5–6; as communications network, 50; creative innovation within, 199–201; decentralized vs. pyramidal, 101; declining (permanent), 183–185; declining (temporary), 185–189; defined, 3; growing, 176–180; indoctrination and socialization policies, 141–144; internal conflicts, 167–174; love-hate relationship between leader and followers, 9–12; market pressures and, 185–189; measuring performance of, 126–127; misorientation in, 72, 139–140; organizational crises, 7–8, 43–47; orientation to, 139–140; output limitation in, 108–111; as quasi-machines, 91–92; stable, 180–182; theory of, 67–68; *see also* Change, organizational; Communication; Management; Managerial succession; Market pressures; Morale; Performance on job; Personnel; Planning, systematic; Productivity; Recruitment policies; Supervision; Tables of organization; Technology

Output quotas, 108–111
Outside experts: functions of, 70–71; and systematic planning, 206

Parkinson, Prof., 57, 184
Parkinsonitis, 184
Patterns of Industrial Bureaucracy (Gouldner), 13
Performance on job: consistency in performance, 145–47; employee performance record (table), 154–155; evaluating, 126–127, 144–153; evaluating: pitfalls to avoid, 152–153; individual performance vs. team performance, 147–148; invisible performances, 151–152; rating systems, 148–151; supervisory reports on, 148
Personal assistants, 21, 23–24
Personnel: headquarters staff, 21, 24–26; perceptions of justice and injustice within organization, 157–167; training and indoctrination of, 137–144; *see also* Conferences; Morale; Performance on job; Rank and file; Recruitment policies; Subordinates; Supervision; Tables of organization; Turnover rates
Planning, systematic, 201–206; and available resources 205; and con-

tradictions in goals, 204; defective planning, 204–206; essential elements in, 203; and information retrieval, 204; master plans, 205; and outside experts, 206; and self-appraisal, 203–204
The Politics of Bureaucracy (Tullock), 28
Population shifts: effect on organizations, 189–190
The Practice of Management (Drucker), 26
Principles of Organization (Caplow), 1
Productivity, 4, 90–127; cheating and, 111–114; of declining organizations, 184; human relations and, 108–111; improving work methods, 106–108; increasing productivity, 106–119; maximizing productivity through indirect supervision, 104–126; measuring, 126–127; motivations for output quotas among employees, 108–111; potential productivity estimates, 104–105; quality control, 119–123; supervision and, 92–104; work flow problems, 114–119; yardsticks of performance, 90–91
Punishments, *see* Rewards and punishments

Quality control: correcting failures in, 121; measures of quality, 122–123; vs. volume of production, 119–120

Rank and file, 30–32; consultations with, 56–57
Rating systems for job performance, 148–151
Recruitment policies: determining essential job qualifications, 131–132; drawn-out procedures, 136–137; explaining job to candidate, 134; indoctrination and socialization of recruits, 141–144; morale and, 129–137; number of candidates, 133–134; sources of information about candidates, 134–136; training recruits, 137–144
Relations in Public (Goffman), 38
"The Reluctant Organization and the Aggressive Environment," 176
Reports, routine: improving quality of, 50–55; sample report, 52
Revenues, declining, 188–189